The Gift

A MADD MOTHER'S JOURNEY *of* HEALING

Margaret Miller

NIMBUS
PUBLISHING

Twenty-five percent of the author's royalties from *The Gift* will go to MADD Canada in the fight against impaired driving and victim support programs.

Nimbus Publishing Limited

PO Box 9166, Halifax, NS B3K 5M8

(902) 455-4286 www.nimbus.ca

Printed and bound in Canada

Library and Archives Canada Cataloguing in Publication

Miller, Margaret, 1954 May 13-
The gift : a MADD mother's journey of healing / Margaret Miller.
ISBN 978-1-55109-825-8

1. Miller, Margaret, 1954 May 13-. 2. MADD Canada—Employees—Biography. 3. Drunk driving—Canada—Prevention. 4. Children—Death.
5. Grief. I. Title.

HE5620.D75C3 2011   363.12'514092   C2010-908146-3

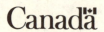
The Canada Council
for the Arts

Le Conseil des Arts
du Canada

NOVA SCOTIA
Tourism, Culture and Heritage

We acknowledge the financial support of the Government of Canada through the Book Publishing Industry Development Program (BPIDP) and the Canada Council, and of the Province of Nova Scotia through the Department of Tourism, Culture and Heritage for our publishing activities.

Nimbus Publishing is committed to protecting our natural environment. As part of our efforts, this book is printed on 100% recycled content paper.

Mixed Sources
Product group from well-managed forests,
controlled sources and recycled wood or fiber
www.fsc.org Cert no. SW-COC-000952
© 1996 Forest Stewardship Council
FSC

This book is dedicated to Bruce
and to the brave families who have shared their stories.

Contents

CHAPTER 1

The Call

I was blessed. My fiftieth birthday was just a few days away and my family had planned a surprise party. My husband, Robert, and our two daughters, Monica and Jeanette, had worked hard to make this a birthday I'd never forget. They made sure that all our friends and family were invited and called Bruce, our youngest child and only son, expecting him to drop everything and be there. Bruce was a police officer in Springhill, Nova Scotia, almost two hours away. Unfortunately, he had already made plans; he was involved with hunting dogs and there were competitions in PEI that weekend. There were lots of calls back and forth as his sisters tried to convince him to come. He was stubborn as usual and I'm sure that the girls had a few choice comments for him, but Bruce had plans and changing them was not an option.

Bruce called to wish me a happy birthday and when he told me about his weekend plans he sounded so excited that I masked my disappointment and told him to have a great time. Bruce promised that he'd be home for a visit soon. I believed him. I had no reason not to.

I said goodbye to my son, not knowing it would be the last time I'd ever hear his voice. I got to say goodbye, but I didn't tell him how much I loved him or how very proud we were of him. I knew there would be a tomorrow, and I was right. That tomorrow came and it's a day we'll never forget.

The party was a huge success. Our home was filled with friends and family, Robert and the girls were proud that they had been able to keep their secret, and the beautiful May evening was filled with good food and rock and roll. As we fell wearily into bed around midnight I felt blessed to have such a wonderful family and great friends. Monica and some of our closest friends from the city had opted to spend the night.

At 3:00 a.m. the phone rang. Nothing good comes from a 3:00 a.m. call. My heart was pounding in my chest as I heard Robert answer, the alarm growing in his voice. I could grasp bits and pieces of the conversation. Something was wrong with Bruce, I gathered that much. Robert told the caller that we were on our way and I reached for my clothing.

"What's going on?" I asked as Robert tossed back the covers and jumped out of bed.

"There's been an accident. Bruce is being taken to the hospital. We need to get there right away."

As I hurriedly dressed, Robert ran into the living room. "Get up!" he screamed at the sleeping household. "We have to go!" His voice was bordering on hysterical. Bedroom doors opened as everyone awoke. "We have to go, right now!"

I tried to calm Robert down and get the rest of the facts. Deputy Police Chief Dean Ruddick had called from Springhill to say that Bruce had been involved in a head-on crash in PEI and was being taken to the Charlottetown hospital. He had serious head injuries and we needed to get there right away.

We called Jeanette at her home just a few miles away, and she answered almost immediately. (Later we learned something strange. She had planned to sleep in that morning and had turned off all the phones in the house. How did she hear the phone or know to pick it up?) Jeanette was on her way to come with us while her husband made arrangements for their children's care and promised to join us soon at the hospital. Meanwhile, Monica called the Charlottetown hospital to see if Bruce had arrived yet. They told her he had arrived and been evaluated, and was being transferred by ambulance to the Moncton hospital, about two hours from our home, where there was a neurology unit.

Our house was scrambling, my head filling with organization details. *Call Rachel, Bruce's fiancée. She's at her parents' home. Wait for Jeanette to get here. Think of what we need. Meds, clothes. We might have to stay a while.*

In no time at all we left our home, but it seemed then that everyone was moving at a snail's pace. Finally, we went out into the dark May night. The sky had never looked so black, so dark, so threatening as we got into two vehicles and drove away.

So festive only a few hours before, our evening had turned into a nightmare.

Robert rode in the back seat of our SUV with our daughters and I was in the front. Our friend Susan Fraser was driving. Others followed in a second vehicle.

Robert had realized the seriousness of the crash. He had heard the voice of the deputy chief, solemn and pained as he delivered his message. I had never before heard the sounds that were coming from my husband—not a cry but a keening, something that I would not even have described as human.

"We've lost our son." It became his mantra, over and over again. I tried to shut out the sound of his voice and refused to believe Robert's prediction. *No way*, I thought. *Bruce is 6'3" and 240 pounds. He is an athlete. No one could hurt him.* I refused to believe anything else, but my panic was close to the surface as I thought about our son and what we might face in the coming hours. I tried to focus straight ahead on the lines on the road. *Make him all right*, I pleaded silently to the dark night, hoping that someone was listening. I thought back to the last time I'd seen Bruce, a few weeks earlier. I hugged him before he left for Springhill on his motorcycle. It was like hugging a brick wall. In my mind I could still feel that hug.

I kept saying to myself, *He'll make it. Brain injuries are survivable. He'll be all right.* I couldn't bear the thought of anything else.

Robert's voice came from the back seat. "We've lost our son."

That two-hour ride seemed to take forever, and my mind wandered into the past. I thought about our family and what had brought us to this point in our lives. I thought about our son and the boy he had been. I tried not to think about what was at the end of the road for us this night. I prayed that my husband was wrong.

✳ ✳ ✳

The thought of turning fifty didn't bother me. After all, I was right where I wanted to be in life.

Life was good—no, it was great. Five years before, in 1999, Robert and I had retired after farming for twenty-five years. We were nineteen and twenty-three when we started. We had lived through many tough and lean years since, and we decided to retire and enjoy ourselves. Selling the farm was our millennium gift to each other.

Retirement was wonderful for the first while. We got up when we wanted to, and our biggest decision of the day was what to cook for dinner or which movie to watch that evening.

We had just built our dream home, and had our own little bit of heaven on earth. But even Eden eventually loses its appeal, and after a year of puttering around with the final details of our new home, Robert decided to go back to his roots and started a small logging business. That suited me just fine. I wasn't accustomed to having him underfoot all the time and although I loved his company, it was nice to see him leave in the morning, knowing I had the day to myself.

We had been together since I was sixteen and he was twenty. We married two years later. I had found my soulmate, the man of my dreams.

Two years after that we had our first child, Monica, followed eighteen months later by Jeanette, and then to everyone's delight twenty-two months later along came Robert Bruce, whom we called Bruce. Those first years were challenging, with the farm and three young children, but we had the energy, drive, and determination to make it work.

People thought we were crazy, and maybe we were, but in the end our vision and hard work paid off.

In 2004, with all three children settled in their own lives, we thought we had no reason to worry.

Monica, our oldest daughter, was thirty that year. Monica is an overachiever, and once she sets her sights on a goal, nothing can stop her. She was working as a massage therapist and was quickly building her clientele. We knew that Monica would deal with her clients as she did everything else: with perfection in her craft and attention to detail. She was an excellent therapist and we had no concerns about her future.

Jeanette, only a year and a half younger than Monica, had taken a totally different path. She was married to a quiet young man, Craig, whom we all grew to love and respect. Her foremost goal was to become a mom and she did just that. First came Austin in 1998, and just a few years later she made us proud grandparents again when she gave birth to Paige.

She was happy and that made us happy. It certainly helped that she lived only a few kilometres away so we saw our grandchildren often.

Bruce we didn't see as much, because he had chosen a life in law enforcement in a small town in northern Nova Scotia, Springhill.

Bruce was one of those farm kids who had lived a charmed life, although with all the responsibilities and farm chores, I'm sure his teenage self didn't agree. His summer days were spent riding his dirt bike, fishing, driving the tractor, or hanging out with his dad. He was independent and smart, and with his inquisitive mind, he was always a parenting challenge.

School was a problem; Bruce hated it. After the first week of primary, Bruce came home one day, crossed his little arms in front of his chest with defiance, and said that he wasn't going back. His dad needed him at home and since he was going to become a farmer he didn't need to go to school. He just wanted to help his dad.

Needless to say, he didn't win that battle, but his attitude towards school didn't change much in the ensuing years.

The day Bruce graduated from high school, his smile said it all. He was done with school and was looking forward to the future, even if he hadn't decided what that future was going to be.

Bruce had very high expectations of the people around him. He was honest, both in action and opinion, and that honesty combined with his quirky sense of humour made those around him take notice. His wit was dry and his comments often sharp and to the point. The only thing he wouldn't tolerate was dishonesty, and I guess that was what led him to his mission in life.

One fall evening in 1998, Bruce was in a neighbouring village visiting a friend. There were a few kids hanging around that day, and one of them said he had to pick up something in a nearby parking lot.

They all decided to tag along, but when Bruce found out that the boy was actually buying drugs, he turned and left.

At home Bruce was furious, and he ranted and raved about what could have happened. I had seldom seen him so angry. Although we didn't approve of the kids' actions, we were a little more tolerant. After all, it wasn't our child buying drugs, so we felt it wasn't our business. I was joking when I told him that maybe he should become a cop.

A few weeks later, Bruce came and told us that I was right, that he should be a police officer.

The search started for a training program and Bruce found that his best chances rested at the Atlantic Police Academy in Summerside, PEI. The application process was long and arduous. There were so many things he needed—a certain swimming level, typing proficiency, defensive driving, and much more—and he only had a few weeks to get everything together in order to be accepted into the next session. He was optimistic, and for the first time really had to work for something he wanted. It was wonderful to see the light in his eyes each morning as he contemplated his future.

Meanwhile, I contacted a friend in the justice system and found out that the police academy had only a few spots, and competition was fierce. Only about one in fourteen applicants were accepted, and of those most were older than Bruce and had applied and been rejected several times before their acceptance.

We gave Bruce the discouraging news, but it didn't deter him from his goal. In fact, he seemed even more determined to succeed. He was invited to try out for the physical testing. As a runner, boxer, and athletic farm boy, he wasn't too worried about this aspect of the testing, passing easily even though a third of the applicants failed.

Now his fears set in. The aptitude testing was notorious for its difficulty. He was told there was a lot of math involved and this panicked him. Math was never one of Bruce's strong points. On the morning of the test we were all in the dairy barn when Bruce said that he had decided not to go for the testing.

I couldn't believe it. The son who wanted to be a police officer so badly was giving up, and to me that just wasn't acceptable. How could he let go of his dream so easily? I cry when I'm upset, and that day was no exception. He stood silently as I said, "I know that you're scared of failing, but if you don't try this you will always wonder if you could have made it. The only way that you'll fail is if you don't try at all."

I walked away from my son and went to the house. My heart was breaking for him. I knew how much he had hoped to get into policing. I was disappointed and wiped away my tears, but had to accept his decision.

A few minutes later Bruce came in and got ready to leave. He didn't say a word as he passed by me. I was ecstatic that my words had hit home, but hid my smile. With a hug and best wishes he was out the door and on his way.

He came home with a big grin on his face. The test wasn't nearly as bad as he had expected. A short time later he learned that he'd passed. There were only two more hurdles: the psychological testing and the final interview.

A burly ex-police officer came to the farm to meet our family and to talk to Bruce. He stressed to us the danger in police work and asked if we were afraid of this career choice. No, we weren't concerned at all. After all, Bruce was capable and careful and there is no place more dangerous to grow up than on a farm. Bruce had spent his life with heavy equipment and thousand-pound, unpredictable animals. I was sure that Nova Scotia streets were no more dangerous.

The officer left that day after telling us all that he thought Bruce would make a wonderful cadet and looked forward to seeing him again as a police officer. I can't tell you how happy Bruce was when he was invited to report to the Atlantic Police Academy. He thought the hard part was over, but it had barely begun.

There were six hundred applicants that year from Nova Scotia, and only fourteen were accepted. These young men and women were an elite group of cadets on the path to their dreams. But that path led through a nightmare of intense training.

Bruce was excited the day he left for the academy, and so were Robert and I. We'll always remember the moment he drove his packed truck down the lane to his future.

We heard from Bruce the next day and his voice cracked with feeling. He sounded tired and at the brink of tears as he told us about his night from hell. He told us that all of the cadets had arrived the evening before and been briefed. Then they were shown exactly how to keep their quarters, including the bed, and all their gear. It had taken him several tries and once his training officer had thrown the bed at him, demanding that he do it right! My normally sloppy son was panicked.

The entire squad had to master the task before anyone could go to bed. They were learning early to work as a team. It was one in the morning when their weary bodies hit the mattresses, and just four hours later they were roused for a five-kilometre run.

After breakfast a day of testing in the classroom began. Bruce had never studied for a test in his life and now had to make eighty percent or above or be expelled from the program.

working on or excited because he was seeing a new girl. Sometimes he would be upset because of something at work or he'd be sad or discouraged, especially if there had been a suicide or something else equally disturbing in town. He knew he could call and be our son, our little boy, instead of Constable Miller, the tough cop who could handle anything, the shoulder everyone else could cry on. Sometimes, he too needed a shoulder.

Bruce loved his job and often said that every day at work was a new adventure just waiting to happen. He had found his place in the world.

One day I was cooking supper and in a bit of a hurry when Bruce called. I tried to get him to call back but he said he just wanted to thank us. I paused.

"Thank us? What do you mean?"

"I just wanted to thank you for being such great parents. You always knew where we were and made sure that we got home on time. You knew what we were doing and you cared. Some of these kids in town are just being dropped off by parents who don't know or care what the kids are doing and they don't care when they come back. I just wanted to call and say thank you."

I thanked Bruce for calling and relayed the conversation to Robert. "He's growing up," I said to my husband. That one call would come to mean more to us than we could have ever guessed.

Days and then years passed for Bruce and he was firmly settled in Springhill. He was in a relationship with a lovely girl and began looking for a home.

Bruce asked Robert and me to come and see a house that he had found and was hoping to buy. It was a cute little place, exactly what he needed. It had lots of room and a small yard for the family he was planning and for his new bloodhound puppy. On February 12, 2004,

Bruce took possession of his new home. It was a huge step for him and the start of a new chapter in his life. By the time he got settled in, spring was in the air, he was happy, and his future was looking bright.

CHAPTER 2

The Nightmare

As we approached Moncton the sun was starting to come up. We could see the flashing lights of an ambulance pulling into the emergency bays as we parked our vehicles. What were the chances it could be him? But it was and we watched Bruce being wheeled in on a stretcher with bags and tubes and attendants everywhere.

We tried to get close to our son, but were blocked by hospital personnel who asked that the doctor be allowed to evaluate him first. The hospital chaplain was in a tiny waiting room and we sat and prayed together that Bruce's life would be spared and that God would be watching over us. It seemed like forever before the doctor came to us. Nothing could have prepared us for his words.

"We're 99.5 percent sure that he is brain dead. We will do more testing, but you should think about organ donation."

Somehow I didn't absorb the "99.5" part, and clung to the remaining "0.5," that little bit of hope we had left. I just kept thinking, *Bruce will make it. He has to. He's strong, he's invincible. He can beat this. Someday we'll laugh about all of this. Bruce will be okay!*

A little later the doctor returned and told us that there was some blood flow to Bruce's brain. That was the good news we had been waiting to hear. He said that Bruce had many broken bones, but they could be fixed. It was the brain injury that concerned them, and if he did recover he might be a quadriplegic. The next few hours were crucial.

We saw our son for a few moments before he was taken to the neurology unit, and then we were directed to a different floor. A different, bigger waiting room. We watched the clock on the wall as it moved ever so slowly.

The room started to fill with Bruce's friends and fellow police officers as word of the crash spread. Soon we, the close family, were allowed to be with Bruce and hold his hand. Surprisingly, he didn't look bad, lying there. He looked like Bruce, but he was so still.

We gathered around his bed and talked to him, pleading with him to wake up and prove the doctors wrong. We begged God to make him well again, to spare our son. I kept wiping away the blood seeping from his right eye as he lay there under a blue plastic sheet designed to keep his broken and bruised body warm.

The noise of the machines in the background was a constant reminder that Bruce was not able to breathe alone. He was being kept alive by those machines.

Monica held his hand a told him that if he woke up she wouldn't tease him about being obese anymore. The nurse looked up as she said those words. It was a private joke that when Bruce went for his physical his doctor told him that with his height to weight ratio he was classified as obese. Bruce was a big man, but certainly not obese! The nurse confirmed this when she said. "There's no fat on that body, we checked him out!" Bruce would have had a big grin on his face if he had been able to hear her. It was a light moment in that terrible day.

We kept vigil around Bruce's bed most of the day, spending odd moments in the waiting room or walking the halls. People were waiting all around us, talking in hushed voices, remembering good times gone by, remembering Bruce and hoping there would be more stories to add to the memories.

Some details of that day are still clear and unforgettable. Some are vague, and I'm sure there is much that I don't remember. At that point I still hadn't succumbed to panic but instead built an emotional cocoon around Bruce and my husband and daughters, trying to keep us from harm.

The day passed as Bruce's friends came forward to say how sorry they were and to find out how he was. We talked to Bruce's friend Steven, who was also a police officer. They shared a love of hunting dogs and Steven told us a little more of what had happened just hours before.

Apparently, Bruce and his friend Jason had been out doing their nighttime trials with their hunting buddies and fellow competitors and they were all headed back to the lodge shortly after one o'clock in the morning. They had stopped in a church parking lot and rearranged passengers to give Bruce and Jason a little more room. Just back on the road, the first truck saw a car speeding towards them. Then they watched, helpless, as the car lost control and slammed into the truck behind them, the one carrying our son and Jason.

They called 911 and responders were there in a matter of minutes. Jason lost consciousness for only a short time and looked up to see Bruce close his eyes for the last time. He began to scream to the attending officer that his friend was a cop and they needed to get him out. The officer stayed with Bruce every moment and even drove the ambulance while the paramedics worked to keep our son alive. Jason watched as they removed Bruce from the truck, wondering if he would ever see his friend again.

Shortly after Steven recounted this to us, doctors came and told us that there was only one more test the hospital could do for Bruce—a brain scan—and that they hoped it would give us some answers.

They cleared Bruce's hospital room as the doctor, an older man, administered the test. We paced the hallways and waited in the family room. There was nowhere we could get away from this nightmare.

Robert overheard the doctor as he barked to no one in particular, "Do I have a witness for this?" He came back to the family waiting room and sat, holding my hand, already knowing the worst.

The nurse came and asked us to get everyone together. The waiting room filled with friends, family, and the Springhill police officers. Some were reluctant to come in, but I think that somehow we believed there was security in numbers. The doctor faced a solemn group as he told us the news.

"We have done the tests. There is no brain activity."

I remember asking, "So, what do we do now?"

He replied with little or no emotion, "I have signed the death certificate." He paused for a moment. "Have you decided about organ donation?"

It was over. Our son was dead. The little hope we had had slipped from our grasp. I thought I heard someone else moaning…keening…sobbing. But in reality it was coming from deep inside me. I know if I hadn't been sitting I would have fallen to the ground. Robert and I continued to hold each other as people quietly left the room and the hospital.

Some stayed to make sure we were all right. I'm sure many said nice, appropriate things, but I can't remember a single one of them.

It was then that we heard the whispers from Bruce's friends, his fellow police officers. They had already been asking questions and they knew….

The driver, the one who had caused the crash, was suspected to have been drunk.

A drunk driver! I couldn't believe it!

The very thing that Bruce worked so hard to stop in his own community had cost him his life and us our son. The driver had also killed himself in the crash.

A very recent memory crept into our grief. One night as I was cooking supper just a week before, the phone had rung.

Robert answered and listened patiently. "Sorry, not at this time," he said, and he returned to the table, telling me that it was Mothers Against Drunk Driving, asking for a donation. How ironic to think of those words while we stood in the hospital. I wondered, *If I had made a donation, would this still have happened?*

Today, in a more reasonable state of mind, I know that it wouldn't have changed anything. But on May 16, 2004, it was all I could think. Because now, I had become a Mother Against Drunk Driving, though certainly not by choice.

We said our goodbyes as we stood around Bruce's bed for a final prayer. I looked down at Bruce in the hospital bed and stood on the spot where I had spent the day hoping for the best. The son that lay there before me was a shell. His heart was beating, being kept alive by technology, but I had to remind myself that he was gone.

Someone said that he had gone to a better place.

There is no better place than in his mother's arms, I thought. *How can this have happened to us? How can we just leave him here?*

The hospital had become a quiet place, the halls all but deserted. And we had to leave our son and walk away. The nurses were waiting to prepare Bruce for organ donation. It was time to leave.

Our legs felt like lead. It was one of the hardest things we had ever done, but we had to go home. There were calls to make, a funeral to arrange. Our son to bury.

I vividly remember walking outside on that beautiful day in May. The sun was shining, the birds singing. People were walking and talking like nothing had happened. It seemed like such a betrayal. Bruce had died, our lives were torn apart, and yet life had gone on around us. I wanted to scream at everyone, "How can you be so happy? Don't you know what's happened?"

The drive back was not hurried. I was so exhausted I could barely stay upright and watched as the trees and hills of the countryside passed by.

When we got back to our home, the driveway was again full of cars—the same scenario as the evening before. Just twenty-four hours before, friends had been there to help us celebrate; now they were there to help us grieve the loss of our child.

Hugs and kisses, tears, solemn voices, coffee, tea. "You have to eat something." "Be strong." And then something special happened. Someone said, " Remember when Bruce…" and the rest of the evening was spent with the memories. Funny, happy memories. It became a celebration of Bruce.

Eventually everyone left, and once again Robert and I were alone with our thoughts. We tried to get some sleep, and with our arms around each other fell into an exhausted abyss.

We woke often through the night, only to burst into tears and once again cry ourselves to sleep. It was a pattern that was often repeated in the weeks that followed.

The next days all ran together in preparation for Bruce's funeral. Thank goodness for the Springhill police and all their help.

Who ever imagines in their worst nightmares that they will have to pick out a coffin for their child, or even decide whether to bury or cremate? What family thinks about burial plots when all is well and you have such hope for the future? We certainly hadn't.

What songs to play, what paper to use, what poems to read, what guestbook, how many flowers to order? But those details kept our minds busy, and in those days, busy was a good thing. Monica and Jeanette helped us decide everything.

We had to choose what Bruce would wear and what would be in the coffin with him forever. I immediately thought of his quilt. A few years before, I had taken up quilting. Bruce was one of those rare men that really appreciated that kind of thing. After my first successful quilt he had asked me to make one for him.

I picked some nice greens and beiges and went to work. In no time at all I had Bruce's quilt ready. He loved it and wherever he lived, the quilt was always on his bed. Bruce called to chat one evening and told me that a young lady had come to his house in Springhill and made a comment about the quilt. She asked Bruce if his "Mommy" had made it for him. Bruce had said yes and asked if she had a problem with that. She didn't last long.

After his death I heard from another special girlfriend, Mandy, who had lived with Bruce for a while. She told me that she had wanted to buy a duvet for the bed. His only comment had been, "You mean for under my quilt?" She didn't buy the duvet.

It was agreed that in his final resting place Bruce would wear his full dress uniform, and tucked around him would be his quilt.

Those days passed quickly. Our home was full of friends, police, and family trying to look after us and help us in our grief. Friends came early in the morning and talked to us until we fell wearily into bed at night. Mornings were the worst. I would wake up as usual, ready to face the day, and then the memories would come and with them the crushing pain. I'd have to stop and try to remember how to breathe again. I'm sure that it was no easier for Robert or the girls. Each of us grieved differently, but we all grieved deeply.

Through it all, I kept thinking about that call from Mothers Against Drunk Driving, and I checked the MADD Canada website. I saw their mission statement to stop impaired driving and support victims of this violent crime. At the time I thought that Bruce and of course Jason were the only victims of this crash, but I read on and began to wonder if I was perhaps a victim too. Maybe MADD could help us, Bruce's family, as well. I took note of the number and put it on my mental "To Do Later" list.

Our home had always been a sanctuary to us. Now, I wandered from room to room, trying to retrieve that peace. I sat in Bruce's old bedroom and tried to feel his presence. A smell, anything…I went to Monica's room, our guestroom, and sat on the edge of her bed. Looking towards the corner I saw an unfamiliar bag and reached for it.

A scream of pain rushed to my throat as I pulled Bruce's overalls, shirt, and boots from the bag. They were all covered with the Bruce's dried blood. I held them to my heart as for the first time I acknowledged the real violence of his death and imagined the scene that terrible night and what our child had gone through. I knelt on the floor, holding his clothing close to me, crying for the son I would never hold again.

Our family always knew that policing was a special family, but never is that more obvious than when that family loses one of its own.

The police were everywhere—our home, the funeral home, and keeping vigil at Bruce's side. Our small community had never seen so many police cars. We were very eased and comforted by the respect and consideration shown by officers from all over the province and even across the country. Tributes and cards began to arrive by the hundred. We valued, appreciated, and cherished every single one.

But they didn't keep the day we dreaded from coming. We had made arrangements to go to the funeral home before the service for a private moment with Bruce before we closed the coffin permanently. A few very close friends and family came—those who had driven us to the hospital and stayed with us that week. It was a solemn time, for we knew that after the casket was closed we'd never see our son's handsome face again. I ran my fingers through his hair as I had in the previous days, and touched his chest and face. He looked so perfect, so at peace. We each said our prayers and final goodbyes.

All around Bruce were mementoes from family and friends. Jeanette left a picture of her children near Bruce's heart, asking him to watch over them and keep them safe.

Monica said her goodbyes in her own way, with quiet reserve.

It was time. Robert and I said our goodbyes. Had our last look, our last touch. There was only one more thing I could do for Bruce, and I covered our son in his quilt to keep him warm in the cold Nova Scotia ground. Our despair was overwhelming, our hearts breaking, as we left the funeral home knowing that the day had barely begun and the worst was still ahead.

The house was full of activity. Preparation for the reception after the funeral was underway and some wonderful friends, Dorthea and Thelma, had agreed to take on this task. I left things in their capable hands.

I had to get away, to escape for a bit from the bustle. I wondered how we would make it through the funeral. How do you survive burying your child? It was well beyond anything I could comprehend. I found my daughters, who were in Monica's room upstairs. We talked quietly, gathering our strength.

Some people will believe the next part of our experience, and some…won't. I believe it. At the hospital as we were getting ready to leave, the nurse had given Jeanette some of Bruce's personal effects—his wallet, watch, and cellphone. In the days following the crash, Jeanette had tried to start the phone with no success. She was concerned that someone might be trying to call or text Bruce and wanted to spare us a shock. After a few days she gave up and dropped the phone into her handbag.

We were waiting for the limo to arrive to take us to the funeral when suddenly we heard a noise. Jeanette opened her bag and picked up Bruce's phone. It was all lit up and the message on the screen said "READY." At the time we just thought it an eerie coincidence—it wasn't until later that Jeanette told us how she'd been unable to turn the phone on. All I know is that at that moment a sense of peace settled around us. We knew we would get through the day, and yes, we were ready. I believe that Bruce was telling us that he was ready as well.

We were warned that many would be there for the funeral, but the reality was overwhelming. The funeral home that seated 450 was full and the parking lot and street were filled with those who had come to pay their respects. The music began as we were ushered into our places and took our seats before Bruce's closed casket. The minister was Reverend Likely, an Anglican pastor from Springhill. Bruce had worked with him, and since he was the police chaplain, it seemed only fitting that Reverend Likely say the words that would dedicate our son's remains to the Lord.

Several of Bruce's friends and fellow officers took part in the service and paid tribute to Bruce. Some with poetry, some with funny stories, but all with love and a deep sense of loss. Monica had asked to do the eulogy and her words shook us all. She spoke of her younger brother, her only brother, with words that made him come to life and that expressed so eloquently the depth of our loss. She ended with a poem that she wrote for Bruce. Her words spoke of their special bond, how much she loved him and would miss him. I was so proud of her and know that Bruce was as well. We felt Bruce all around us that day and as the final song played, Rod Stewart's "Forever Young," we followed the casket from the funeral home.

I had no expectations, so to come onto the street in our small village and see the hundreds of officers standing side by side along the street's edge, hands in salute as we passed, was amazing. It was a sight we'll never forget.

Our limo followed the hearse a few short miles to Bruce's burial place. All along the route, wherever there was an intersecting road, there stood a police car with members standing at attention when we passed. I'll always remember the RCMP officer saluting as we passed, tears streaming from his eyes.

We congregated around the spot that we as a family had selected for Bruce's final resting place. Everything was ready and Reverend Likely said his words of committal. I can't even remember the words, but the thing that stood out was the final call. Through a police radio we heard "Code Three, Officer Down, Officer Down," and then silence. There was no help for this officer, our son, Bruce.

Soon all the officers passed by us offering condolences. Many were openly crying; all were touched by Bruce's death. I expect we shook hands with each and every one and thanked them for coming, though

I can't say for sure. So much of that day was shrouded in a deep fog and a self-protecting numbness that allowed us to function outwardly. We were aware, but on many levels, we weren't even there.

Thank goodness for the friends who stood close by and would stay close by in the days and years ahead. We would need them desperately.

CHAPTER 3

Getting Madd

Busy days were best. They passed quickly. Though we never stopped thinking, our days became bearable. But each night as we lay in bed our grief was raw and open, and it took a long while before I stopped crying myself to sleep.

Robert patiently consoled me, but I knew how much he felt the grief and loss of our son as well. They say that time helps, but in those days, we wouldn't have believed it.

In the meantime, I had gone back to the MADD Canada website. I read more about this organization and grew to appreciate what they were doing. I found the number for victim support and called, not knowing what to expect. I left a voicemail with my name and number. A short while later a woman named Gloria Appleby called back and talked to Robert. He spoke to her that first time and told her a little about what had happened. I called back soon after. I can't even say what I expected or that I expected anything. I told Gloria that our son had been killed by a drunk driver the week before. She didn't push for information, but said, "Tell me about Bruce."

A floodgate opened as I told her about our son, his hopes and dreams, and what had happened to destroy our lives.

I'm sure I ranted and raved to this wonderful woman and probably demanded that something be done. She listened and heard me voice all my pain and frustration. She asked about our family and the support system we had in place. When I asked her how often this happened she told me that we were the fourth family to call who had lost family members that same weekend. I couldn't believe it. I later learned that one of those families was also from Nova Scotia. A woman and her fiancé had been killed in Cape Breton.

Gloria told me that 4 people were killed each day in Canada and 196 were injured. Impaired driving was the leading criminal cause of death in Canada. The numbers were shocking and staggered me. Now I knew why MADD Canada's work was so important. I told her that I had questioned whether I should call. After all, it was Bruce who was the victim, not me. She soon cleared up my misconception. Gloria told me that anyone who has been impacted by impaired driving is considered a victim. Losing our son had certainly put us in that category.

We talked for what seemed like forever. There was no pressure, no hurry, only that voice of calm on the phone. An island of sanity in our new reality, that dark void that had become our lives.

Gloria promised to send me some material that we could use for reference and some other information for our daughters on grieving. She also told me about a MADD Canada chapter in nearby Truro that had just opened and had a Victim Services volunteer. She gave me the contact number and I hung up from that call with a sense of promise. MADD could help us! Although friends and family wanted to, these good people knew exactly what we were going through—many of them had been in our shoes.

The days and weeks passed. All but the closest of our friends went back to their families and their own lives. Robert and I tried hard to make life a little normal again, but that was impossible.

The town of Springhill had asked about having a memorial service for Bruce and of course we agreed. These were the very people he had wanted to help so much, and now they wanted to pay their respects and mourn his loss. A few weeks earlier we had seen an article in the paper, a tribute to Bruce, written by a woman who worked at a Tim Hortons coffee shop across from the police station. She had written some very nice things and I had stopped in to thank her for her words. She shared with me a personal story of how Bruce had helped her family and how much it meant to her.

Needless to say, it made me even more proud of my son and made me appreciate what a caring police officer he had become. After hearing many more such stories, I saw a pattern emerging. Bruce hadn't just talked the talk but had walked the walk and put himself out there for each and every one of these people. He was loved in Springhill and would not be forgotten.

One day I needed to call the Springhill police department about the memorial service and picked up my phone book to call. In the front leaf I had tucked one of Bruce's business cards, which he had left after stopping in unexpectedly and finding no one home. On the card, not knowing how much it would mean to me one day to find it in my phone book, he had written, "I was here!" On the bottom of his card was his work voicemail number. I don't know what made me call, or what I'd hoped to find. I knew he wouldn't answer, that he was gone, but still I dialled the numbers and heard his voice on the line. I can barely describe that moment; it was so shocking to hear his voice. I sobbed hysterically with longing and grief. It was a long while before I was able to pick up the phone again and call Cindy at the police department, and when I finally did, I still couldn't speak. I began to cry into the phone. She must have thought I was having a major meltdown.

I guess that's exactly what it was. I tried once again to call the voice-mail number several months later, but thankfully, the account had been closed.

A month after Bruce's death and the day before the service, we met with Jason for the first time. He wanted to go to the Springhill memorial service but didn't want to upset us—we had never met him before, and he thought that meeting him for the first time under those circumstances would have been impossibly hard for us. Robert and I were touched by this young man who had shared Bruce's last waking moments. Jason seemed to think that there should have been something he could have done to prevent Bruce's death, but we knew better. We were just glad that Bruce had been with someone like Jason and had not been alone on that stretch of highway.

The memorial service in Springhill, held a month after Bruce's death, was moving and touching as some of Bruce's colleagues shared funny stories. The chief and mayor spoke of the loss to the community and our family. By now some of our protective numbing shield had gone, and in many ways this service was even harder than the funeral itself. I wouldn't have thought it possible.

We had had a month with our grief and had somehow thought this memorial would be easier. I was wrong and often without warning, that numbing despair would hit and take us back to that dark place in a millisecond. Every day we missed Bruce more.

The material arrived from MADD Canada and gave me something to read, something concrete to hold. I knew I was doing the right thing when I called the local MADD chapter, MADD Cobequid, and met with the chapter president, Kathleen (Kay) Foster-Alfred. She wanted to support us so much but I didn't want help at that point. I just wanted to do something about drunk driving. I went to the local meeting and knew immediately that it was the one place I could make a difference. I was not ready to jump in with both feet yet, but they gave me the time I needed and I appreciated that.

I thought that MADD was all about moms. I was wrong. One of the first people I met at the meeting was the deputy police chief from Truro, who had been at Bruce's funeral, and who spoke of his respect for Bruce. Then I met others who wanted to make a difference: a local paramedic, a housewife, an RCMP officer, and many more. People from every walk of life with a common mission, MADD Canada's mission: "To stop impaired driving and support victims of this violent crime."

That first meeting I just let it all sink in. They gave me a membership form that highlighted all the different areas in which volunteers could work with MADD. Kay very patiently went over them but added that I could contribute more or less anytime I wished.

There is a public policy category. MADD Canada actively lobbies government officials to make better legislation; there are far too many loopholes in the system that sometimes seems to favour offenders. A volunteer's involvement in this category could be at a very local level, talking to our local MLA or our MP.

Another category described how to become a Victim Support Volunteer, or VSV—a program from which I was benefiting through Kay, a VSV herself, trained in helping victims on their road to healing. It's a complex role that needs specialized training and at that time I was still so needy I knew I couldn't be of help to anyone else. I would, however, benefit from Kay's expertise in the months to come.

Court monitoring, another volunteering possibility, sounded interesting to me. MADD Canada trains volunteers to go into courtrooms and monitor the outcome of impaired driving charges. The role of the court monitor is passive—they just sit, watch, and record—but that small measure has been very effective. It gives MADD information for our records and lets the courts know that the organization is aware of what is happening in courts across the country.

Volunteers can also help with a national poster and essay contest. I learned that school children from across Canada can make a difference by drawing posters or writing real or fictional stories and submitting them for the contest. It's a great way to engage young minds with the message that they too can make a difference. There is also a multimedia aspect to the contest, and older teens can create video or audio submissions. MADD Canada has a whole site dedicated to youth, and youth membership is encouraged.

The Project Red Ribbon program was something I didn't know much about. Kay explained that it was a national event. Chapters and community leaders across the country set up donation boxes and distribute ribbons at sobriety checkpoints. This program is MADD Canada's signature event, intended to create awareness about impaired driving across Canada. I asked Kay what a community leader was. In areas of the country that don't have the volunteer base for a chapter, often a concerned citizen will represent MADD Canada, as they are able, in their community. What a great example of one person making a difference.

The list went on and on. Public education, office support, fundraising, special events, youth initiatives, public speaking, media relations. That one brought me to a halt. No way was I going to work with media. The thought of getting in front of a camera was terrifying.

I came from that meeting a little overwhelmed but feeling good for the first time in a long time. I felt at ease with this group. We shared a common goal.

I was again taking control of my life and the sense of my life spiralling out of control was slowing down. I was now armed with information and conviction.

Later in the week, I was once again at the MADD Canada website looking for victim information. I had already read through the package I'd received about victim support. It was so helpful because it talked about everything in the process, from the funeral to the justice system and grief counselling. I read the online tributes and felt the grief and sharing in those tributes. I knew that grief. I saw photos of the memorial wall on MADD's website and knew that Bruce's photo should be there as well. I sent in a picture and worked on my online memorial. MADD gave me purpose and a direction for my new reality. It was a fragile bit of healing and purpose. But it was a start.

Family occasions were still the toughest. Monica came for one of her rare visits one Sunday and needed a ride back to the city. She didn't spend a lot of time at our house that first summer and I couldn't really blame her. It had become a very sad and sometimes volatile place. I dropped her off at her Halifax apartment and suddenly the pain was all there. It was as if by saying goodbye to her, I was again saying goodbye to Bruce, and it once again hit me how "forever" our loss was. I was paralyzed with grief and couldn't even think about getting behind the wheel of the car. I called Robert at home and between sobs and intense crying, repeated again and again, "Bruce is never coming home and we can't do anything about it."

"I know," Robert kept saying. By now he was frantic with worry. He couldn't come and get me but urged me to calm down and try and get home safely. "Bruce wouldn't want you to be so upset," he said. He was right.

It took a little while before I could drive, and even then my vision was blurred by my seemingly endless tears. Finally I got home and collapsed into my husband's arms. The painful reality of our new lives was becoming alarmingly clear.

It was a long and sad summer. A moment of quiet would lead to memories and then to tears. Friends dropped in less and less often. We would meet people on the street and their well-meaning words often reflected how little they really understood.

"How are you?" they would ask.

How do you think I am? I'm terrible.

"Fine," I'd say.

"You are so lucky that you have other kids."

I'd be lucky if we still had Bruce.

"Yes, we are," I'd say.

"Time will heal," they would say.

Never.

"I hope so," I'd say.

"You can't let this defeat you."

It already has.

"We'll be okay," I'd answer, though I knew we'd never be okay again.

The best support came from friends who were there and just let us talk. People like Sue, who was available day and night whenever I needed to talk; or our Friday night supper friends, Nigel and Kathryn, who always listened. I'm sure they sometimes were tired of hearing the same things every week. But they were and still are there.

By fall, I felt we were coming around a little. Sometimes five whole minutes would go by without us thinking about what had happened. I thought that we must almost seem normal to most people, but then I saw a picture of us at our granddaughter's birthday party in

September, and the looks on our faces showed all our pain and grief. When I look at that photo now, it is all so fresh again. We will never be the same people we were before Bruce's death. That tragedy has changed us forever.

And then there were the times when I questioned if all of this had really happened. Some days I thought that I was losing my mind.

One day I was in the drugstore in our village and happened to glance around. I saw the back of a young man. My heart leapt to my throat. It looked like Bruce! *Could it be him?* I wondered. *I saw the casket close, I held his hand but...is it possible?* I walked slowly towards this young man—but no, of course it wasn't Bruce. I left the store in tears.

Incidentally, I don't believe that these moments are caused only by fresh grief. It happened to me again two years later, on a plane. I saw the back of a head that looked like my son's. It was like a slam to my chest and I started hyperventilating. I knew it wasn't Bruce, and yet still I thought...I made myself stay in my seat and stay calm. My eyes never left that young man and soon I saw him get up for something. It wasn't Bruce and I could breathe easier again.

When I think about the first two months after Bruce's death and the fog of grief that enshrouded me, I remember a particular event that brought me back from that state of bleak despair. It was a moment that I would describe as a turning point and that inspired me to take further action.

The young man who caused the crash that killed Bruce and himself had been going to graduate from Holland College, the same school that Bruce attended, though in another division. His family wanted to start a scholarship fund in his memory to pay tribute to their son—and really, I can understand why they wanted to do something good after all that had happened. But their son was a drunk driver who killed our son and now they wanted to honour him at the same school that trained Bruce as a police officer. To us it was a slap in the face, in total disregard for our feelings, and an insult not only to Bruce's memory but to all police officers. I contacted the school and was assured that the family had not approached the school and that a scholarship would not be set up. A month or so later I followed up and discovered that in fact there was a fund in place.

I objected strongly, but the administrator asked why I would stand in the way of something good coming from the "accident." Then she said, "It's not as if you can do anything about it, anyway."

She didn't know me, or that my silent response was *Just watch me!*

I contacted a few of Bruce's friends who were police officers and they were as outraged as I was. Soon the correspondence was flying through police departments province-wide, and the media began to notice. After I did a very emotional interview on CBC Radio, the family withdrew their application.

No matter what a person does in their life, if they kill while driving impaired, they don't deserve to be honoured. It's that simple—and yes, that tough.

Someone's choice to drive drunk took away the life we loved. We thought that we were good people, and that bad things didn't happen to good people. We thought that our kids were all safe and that Canadian highways were safe for our loved ones to travel. How naïve we were. How innocent. How wrong. No one is safe as long as impaired driving is tolerated by the public.

At the point when the door to our old life was closed forever, a small window opened. MADD Canada held their arms out to us, as they do for all victims. MADD gave us a way to pay tribute to Bruce on their website, at the local Candlelight Vigil of Hope and Remembrance, with roadside memorials, and in many other ways.

Our story wasn't over. In many ways it had just begun.

I learned a lot in the fall of 2004 about MADD Canada and the work they do. As promised, the local chapter president kept me busy. Kay was a one-woman dynamo in the Truro office and asked me to be her vice-president. I jumped at the chance, determined to change the world. There was a petition that needed signatures asking for mandatory prison time for those who kill or do serious injury while driving impaired. I took it with me everywhere and asked friends and neighbours to support our efforts. At that time many convicted offenders received conditional sentences and spent their time at home, doing as they pleased! It was totally unacceptable and the public was outraged. After many attempts, legislation was successfully passed on November 30, 2007, just months after I became national president. That success made me realize that every person has a voice that can be heard. I became determined to do more.

In the spring of 2005, the MADD Canada national multimedia shows began to appear in our local schools. These are impressive video presentations on three screens that span a whole gymnasium. The shows start in September and cross the country, going to as many high schools and middle schools as possible. Each year the show is a new production and lets students meet victims' families and see the results of impaired driving; it's powerful, raw, and emotional.

A local chapter representative usually opens the show, and Kay suggested I share Bruce's story at a small high school in Musquodoboit, Nova Scotia. I agreed to, although I was terrified of speaking before the group of about three hundred students. I found it easy to tell the audience the facts and figures, and had no trouble telling them about the perils of impaired driving. But after I told them I'd lost Bruce less than a year before, I couldn't say more. Just those few words brought a lump to my throat; I could barely say Bruce's name. I wanted to do more, but I wasn't ready yet.

Then a call came to go to a high school in Brookfield. I went thinking I would be handing out MADD ribbons, but when I arrived, the organizers told me I was presenting in five minutes. I looked frantically for the notes I'd used in Musquodoboit, but I couldn't find them. I thought about backing out. Then I remembered how much Bruce wanted to help the kids in his own town. If these students could hear about Bruce and what happened to him, he still could make a difference.

It was all the incentive I needed, and I felt Bruce at my side as I walked onto the stage. I told the students about our son, and how much he wanted to make a difference. Then I told them about the crash and what happened that terrible night, not even a year before. Sometimes the words seemed to get stuck in my throat and I'd need to wait a second before I could go on. Then I'd look at a young, inno-cent face in the crowd and see how intensely they were listening. My words were getting through! This is the story I was meant to tell. The facts and figures are important, but these students needed to hear from someone who could have been their mom as I was Bruce's.

My legs were weak as I left the stage, my heart heavy with the pain of grief. Sobs were lodged in my throat. Someone reminded me to breathe. I knew that these young people would not forget this pres-entation and hopefully, hopefully, just one would remember me when they were in a position to make that choice—drive or don't drive, get in with an impaired driver or make other arrangements. This is the first part of MADD Canada's mission.

To stop impaired driving.

And Bruce and I were making a difference.

* * *

One of the first things that many new victims do is attend the Annual Candlelight Vigil of Hope and Remembrance and Victims' Weekend in Toronto. Robert and I were chosen by the Cobequid chapter to attend, but we didn't realize at the time the impact the weekend would have on our healing. All I knew was that there would be many victims like us at the conference and that the focus was on dealing with grief, among many other related subjects.

The anniversary of Bruce's death was approaching, and it brought with it a sense of escalating emotional desperation. We had thought that we had our emotions somewhat under control. What a joke! The rawness of this returning grief was terrifying, seemingly coming from nowhere. Now we had to meet strangers and live through our loss all over again.

I believe that if the Cobequid chapter had not already paid for our trip, Robert and I would have backed out at the last minute. We left for Toronto full of apprehension and fear. All the conference had asked for in advance was Bruce's picture and a tribute to be read at the candlelight vigil. The chapter paid for all expenses.

A limo dropped us off at the conference site. As we walked into the reception area, I introduced myself. "I'm Margaret Miller and this is my husband, Robert." A tiny lady walked around the desk with her arms open in welcome. "We've been expecting you," she said. "Welcome."

It was Gloria Appleby, the woman who had answered our first desperate call for help. She introduced us to the others and made us feel welcome. Although we didn't know it yet, we had already become a part of the MADD Canada family—a family that would stand by us through the months and years ahead.

The weekend was amazing. For the first time we were with people who knew exactly what we were feeling. They had been there themselves. The speakers knew just what to say and often their words reached us at a level that inspired hope. It was good to feel that maybe there was some hope for our future. We met so many people that were in different stages of the same journey. We were able to look into our future and feel for the first time that we would survive our loss and Bruce's death.

We met one particular couple that weekend that I still think of. They were an older couple, I believe from Ontario. They had lost their son, daughter-in-law, and two grandchildren all in the same crash. They were left with one granddaughter. I remember the couple so well because of the look in the woman's eyes, like she was dead inside, and her husband was trying so frantically to help her. Although I was determined not to be like her, I now recognize that same dead look from the photos of Robert and I from the months after our loss, when the grief was so new and when sometimes the only place to hide was within ourselves. I hope that woman from the conference is in a better place now.

One of the most dramatic things at the conference is the national memory wall, which displays pictures of those killed or injured by impaired drivers. At that time, the wall was on several tables with almost a thousand photographs arranged alphabetically. We read every single name and date, our pain and horror increasing with each one. Everyone was represented, from the very old to those stillborn because of a crash. Finding Bruce's picture among them was a shock, because we now realized that Bruce had joined yet another family. He was a member of the Miller family, the policing family, and now the family of those killed by impaired driving. He didn't deserve to be there. No one did.

The candlelight vigil that weekend was one of the most moving and dramatic events I have ever attended. The national board was led into the ceremony by bagpipers amid a colour guard of police members from all across Canada. A soloist's voice sang out and touched my soul. The event was so like Bruce's funeral. Soon the victims' portraits began to flash across the fifty-foot screen at the front of the room and tributes were read as family members were asked to stand and acknowledge their loved ones. One by one, hundreds of tributes were read, and then Bruce's picture was in front of us and Robert and I rose to our feet. I could barely stand, and I cried as they read our words: "Always loved, forever missed. We will never forget you."

We left the ceremony emotionally drained but feeling strangely better as well. We had become part of this group that understood our loss. The weekend was a turning point for us. I can't say that we were magically healed—we weren't—but it was an experience that made a difference, for we now knew we weren't alone. That in itself provided much-needed solace.

With renewed resolve to do everything I could to keep other families from going through what we had, I jumped into the MADD Canada programs with both feet. At the national leadership conference that fall, I met even more of my MADD family. Not as many victims attended this conference, but the delegates were chapter members who wanted to make their chapters more effective. There was representation from Newfoundland and Labrador to British Columbia and the Yukon. Here we learned the many ways we could influence the public, spread our message, and stop this senseless loss of life. Like me, many of the delegates were victims and had lost family members due to impaired driving. A lot of us had lost children, but some had lost parents or siblings as well.

What really stood out was the number of volunteers who had not suffered a loss but had become involved when they saw a need in their community. How I wish I had been one of them, but it took Bruce's death to open my eyes to what was going on all around me.

I found out that there were 108 chapters and community leaders across Canada, with a total of 7,500 volunteers. I was so proud to be one of them. I also was impressed with the number of police officers involved with MADD Canada. These men and women are on the front lines of our battle against impaired driving and feel that prevention is better than picking up the pieces. I couldn't agree more.

I became familiar with a booklet called "Rating the Provinces," a study of the impaired driving legislation in each province. I was surprised to hear of some provincial laws—like the fact that young people in Alberta can obtain a learner's permit to drive at fourteen. I can't imagine; sixteen still seems very young to have this responsibility.

It was a real eye opener to hear the frustration of volunteers and victims who had been revictimized by a justice system in which all too often an impaired driver who killed or injured someone got sent home to do their time (this being 2005, two years before the mandatory jail-time legislation was passed). Was it any wonder that impaired drivers didn't take their crimes seriously? The need for change became apparent in every session I attended. My only questions were "What's taking so long?" and "Why wasn't this done years ago?" Every single one of MADD Canada's suggestions made perfect sense, and I couldn't understand why all of their proposals hadn't already been enacted.

I was told that some of these measures had been before government for years but that the wheels of justice turn slowly. How many more need to die before someone pays attention? If these changes had been made years ago, would Bruce still be alive? How many have been killed needlessly, how many injured? Who has to die before the public pays attention?

Other than adding more fuel to my fire, the conference also introduced me to a wonderful woman. Her name was Brenda Adams and she, too, was from Nova Scotia. Brenda was in a wheelchair. She was so upbeat, positive, and friendly, I just had to know what had brought her to MADD. I needed to know her story.

CHAPTER 4

Victims Matter

We sat in the lobby of the conference centre in a quiet corner as Brenda told me what had brought her to MADD and put her in her wheelchair.

In the spring of 1991 she had recently moved to Ottawa and found a job with the government. Having lived in rural Nova Scotia, a government job in our nation's capital was her dream come true. Brenda was happy and planning a wonderful, exciting future.

One night she and a friend, Lisha, went to visit Brenda's aunt who lived near Ottawa. After their visit, just a mile from her aunt's home, a twenty-five-year-old man who had decided to leave his stag party was driving home. He was more than a little drunk—Brenda later learned that his blood alcohol content was more than three times the legal limit. He was a disaster waiting to happen. He lost control of his vehicle only five feet away from Brenda, and his truck hit the driver's side of her car, flipped over, and bounced off her car. Brenda's car's sunroof was knocked into her backseat and the truck driver was ejected and actually bounced off Brenda's skull. Brenda has no memory of these moments, but others bear witness to what was happening around her—the carnage, the smell, and the sounds of destruction.

The first person at the scene was a nurse who worked at a nearby school. She checked Brenda and after detecting no pulse went to the aid of Lisha. They thought Brenda was dead. The jaws of life were brought in to remove Brenda's broken body and it was as they were removing her from her car that they heard a moan and realized that she was still alive.

The ambulance took Brenda to the nearest hospital, only to be turned away because of the extent of her injuries—they didn't have the facilities to be able to do anything for her. No one actually expected her to live, and no wonder. Brenda had three skull fractures and a broken nose, and the right side of her face was torn away. She had no sight in her left eye and her neck was broken in three places. Many of her ribs were broken and she had a punctured lung. Her left arm was broken, both hips were broken. Her knees were smashed.

I shook my head in wonder as Brenda told me all this. I couldn't imagine what she had gone through. And yet she was sitting here before me, still willing to continue with her story. And she was smiling!

Brenda was in an induced coma for two days and awoke with total amnesia. She didn't know anyone and could remember nothing about her life.

Four days later doctors started the many surgeries Brenda would have to endure in the attempt to make her whole again. The worst thing for her was the torturous halo brace that surrounded her head to help her neck heal. Told at first that it would be on for four weeks, Brenda had to wear it for sixteen long weeks. Slowly Brenda's memory began to return. Small things acted as triggers until she regained some semblance of what had happened. She asked about her friend and found that Lisha had also suffered serious injuries and wasn't in much better shape than Brenda. But Brenda couldn't think about that. She had to heal herself first.

Brenda spent three weeks in Ottawa General Hospital and then went to a rehabilitation centre where she spent the next eleven months. I can only imagine what those months were like and the pain she must have endured.

Meanwhile, her positive nature refused to allow her to think the worst. She was making the best of a situation that would have crushed most of us. For instance, on Halloween of that year, she had a friend bring her some wings. She wanted to celebrate and the wings, along with her halo brace, turned her into an angel.

Still, even with her positive attitude, rehabilitation was a long and painful process. Brenda had to learn to sit, to feed herself, eventually to dress herself. How many tears were shed as part of that process? I can't begin to imagine the courage it took for Brenda just to wake up each day, knowing all her limitations, knowing that a simple thing like blowing her nose could be a challenge. Those are the things we all take for granted until something like this happens.

Brenda also had to come to terms with what had happened to her. At first she refused to look in the mirror that hospital staff brought to her, but four months later she was finally willing to look at her own face and the extent of her injuries. She didn't know what to expect, but bravely took the mirror in her hands. She could trace the lines of each scar with her eyes, see the healing, see what still needed to heal.

I asked her if she ever felt sorry for herself while in the hospital, and she told me about a girl in her ward who had suffered a stroke as a result of using birth control pills. She only had the ability to move her eyes. She was working with someone to get a law degree. She was so inspirational that Brenda couldn't feel sorry for herself. Two other patients in the ward had been paralyzed, and both had recovered and walked out of the rehabilitation centre. Brenda was determined to do the same.

One day her lawyer came to visit and asked her a strange question. He asked which of her senses she would give up to have her legs back if she had the chance. I can't imagine having to answer that question, but Brenda quickly gave her answer—none.

"I can't walk yet, but I can still see the stars, smell roses, and hear laughter." To her, those were the important things in life. If need be, she could live without her legs.

But her legs were not the only problem. Brenda also has permanent brain damage, causing short-term memory loss. She jokes about it often, and says it can make life interesting!

Brenda also lost many of her old friends. They didn't know what to say or how to talk to someone in a wheelchair. They wanted the old Brenda back, and she didn't exist anymore.

Brenda met her husband, Scott, while in rehabilitation, although they didn't connect at that point. He was just one of the bus drivers, and they didn't have any personal conversations. The centre offered frequent outings and Brenda was anxious to get out and try to resume a normal life. At first she was given a variety of mobile chairs but always refused a wheelchair, still adamant that she wouldn't need one. When she finally "got with the program," as she puts it, she picked out a hot-pink number with lots of cool accessories.

Brenda was ready to be released and luckily had her job waiting for her. But getting back into a social life was much harder. Her self-esteem was low, and for a year and a half she went from one bad relationship to another. It was a very dark time for her, but eventually she realized she needed to make some genuine friends. Brenda began to go for walks, swimming, to the gym, and on the weekends, dancing. She tried everything—skiing, sailing, and even horseback riding. She was happy in her own right and needed no one else in her life to make her feel worthy. Brenda soon became involved with her former bus driver, Scott. They hit it off and became engaged. They both wanted children and to their delight, Brenda became pregnant almost right away. She laughed as she told me how excited they were at the news. I asked her how hard it had been, and whether her family had been concerned about how she would handle raising a child.

"It's true that I'd never had a baby, but he'd never had a mother!" was her reply.

Brenda took all the challenges of raising a newborn in stride—in fact, she says her biggest challenge was convincing other people that she could handle Brandon by herself. Soon they moved back home to Yarmouth, Nova Scotia, to be close to her family, and Brenda continued to prove herself a wonderful mother. Brandon, now a teenager, is a son to be proud of.

Brenda does, occasionally, need help with a few tasks, like mopping floors or dusting furniture that is out of her reach, and her husband and son are happy to help her whenever she will let them! She drives, does the grocery shopping, and much more. Brenda didn't allow the drunk driver to take away her independence—but he did take away the life and dreams of that girl in 1991. Now Brenda has other dreams and finds a way to fulfill each and every one of them.

As Brandon grew, the family of three was busy and generally very happy. But the one thing that continued to bother Brenda was the prevalence of drunk driving in her community. It angered her that so many people thought it acceptable to drink and drive. She knew from experience that a life could be turned upside down because of one person's terrible decision. Was what happened to her not a lesson to the rest of the community?

In 2003 Brenda heard about a local MADD chapter and made some calls. Before long she joined MADD Yarmouth and has since been doing amazing things in her community—she is an inspiration to all of us.

Brenda talks to convicted impaired drivers, sharing her story in the hope that they will never reoffend. She also speaks at schools and wherever she feels she can make a difference. If there is an event in her community, Brenda is likely there with her MADD Yarmouth display, creating awareness and raising money to further their mission.

Brenda spoke to me once of her dreams and said that when she dreams she isn't walking but flying. She is looking down at those who walk and take it for granted. Her flying makes her feel special because she knows she has wings and can go anywhere. She wakes up each day glad to be alive and hoping that she can make a difference in someone else's life.

I am also glad that she is alive to carry her message to all of us. She *is* making a difference in the lives of others, as she has made a difference to me. No doubt our paths will continue to cross often.

Brenda represents only one of the almost seventy thousand new victims injured yearly by someone's decision to drive impaired. Some are not hurt as badly as Brenda, but many sustain even worse injuries. MADD Canada works with the victims and their families, and has produced a book called *Coping with Life After Injury*, available from every local MADD chapter or as a PDF on the MADD Canada website.

Unfortunately, most of the public doesn't realize just how many injury victims there really are. These are in many cases the forgotten multitude. If their voices don't speak to the public, then maybe the cost of their injuries will. Because impaired driving doesn't only cause pain and suffering—it has financial ramifications as well. Between doctors' care, hospital stays, physiotherapy, home care, lost productivity, court costs, incarceration, and so much more, the cost of impaired driving to Canadians is a whopping $12.9 billion a year. Surely that number will incense even the Canadians least concerned about impaired driving.

Many of the people MADD refers to as victims, like Brenda, call themselves survivors instead. One young woman told me that although her injuries may keep her from doing a thousand different things, there are eight thousand things she can still do—and she's only halfway through her list. Her positive spirit is inspiring.

Many survivors speak at schools and talk to teens in a way that really connects. The students can actually see what the effects of drunk driving are from someone who has been there. These survivors are making a difference, changing attitudes and saving lives one person at a time.

* * *

After that leadership conference in the fall of 2005, after meeting Brenda and so many inspiring volunteers, I came home with a renewed sense of purpose, determined to make a difference, to make Bruce's life and even his death count for something. Robert and the girls supported my efforts completely, and Jeanette even joined the chapter. Robert wasn't yet ready to become a member but was there whenever I needed a sounding board or just needed to vent.

MADD Cobequid is a wonderful chapter, and our president, Kathleen Foster-Alfred, had so many terrific ideas that it was easy to keep busy. Often the only thing that stood in our way was the lack of available funds.

One day as Robert and I sat on our veranda, overlooking the property that had been our farm and was now a beautiful golf course, a thought came to my mind. We saw how many people were going up to the golf course and noted how many tournaments were going on. I had heard about a chapter in Ontario that had raised about ten thousand dollars and wondered if we could do the same.

The CST Bruce Miller Memorial Golf Tournament was born that fall, with our first tee-off date set for the first Monday after Fathers' Day in 2006. It would be a family tournament with all funds going to MADD Cobequid for their services and programs. I had no idea what I was doing. I didn't golf and neither did Kay, but sometimes when you come at a project from a different angle, it can actually make it better.

Bruce's tournament was a lot of work, but when we stood on the course that first June day, knowing that so many of Bruce's friends and family were here to pay tribute and remember our son while helping MADD Cobequid, it made it all worthwhile. Robert is not a public speaker, but starting that day and continuing at the tournament every year since, he is the one behind the podium telling a story or two about our son and, yes, he always makes us cry. We feel Bruce with us on the course. These are the fields where he grew up and worked. It is the perfect place to remember our son in this extra-special way each year.

The CST Bruce Miller Memorial Golf Tournament at the Links at Penn Hills, Shubenacadie, grows every year and has in the last five years brought about seventy-five thousand dollars to the chapter. For me it is a labour of love. Thank you, Bruce.

* * *

It was always my intention to give what I could to MADD, but in reality MADD gave more back to me than I could ever have imagined. With every school I visited, and every opportunity to make change I seized, I found myself healing a little more. To see positive change being made is empowering. Yes, we all were the victims of impaired driving, but the driver no longer had any power over me. He had taken enough, and now we were fighting back.

In the fall of 2006 I received a phone call that led to another chance for me to further the fight.

Susan MacAskill is the chapter services manager for the Atlantic provinces. She is also a victim of impaired driving; she lost her dad, Donald King, to a drunk driver. Susan has been a continual inspiration to me. She was one of the first to pursue MADD Canada about opening a chapter in Nova Scotia and started MADD Annapolis Valley. Some people are born leaders and Susan is one of them.

Susan called and asked if I was aware that the national president, Karen Dunham, was due to step down from her volunteer position as MADD Canada's national president in the fall of 2007.

She then asked if I would think of applying for the position. She saw what I had been doing locally and thought that my passion for our mission would serve the organization well on a national scale. She let me see that it would be an opportunity to share Bruce on a national level, and for him to carry on with his mission: to protect and serve. It was an opportunity to become MADD Canada's national spokesperson.

I was terrified but also intrigued. *Could I? Should I?*

It would mean I would be away often, since the position required a fair bit of travel, and I thought that might be a problem. After all, Robert and I had been together for thirty-five years, each and every day, and had never travelled apart. I spoke to Robert about Susan's suggestion and he agreed that I should give it chance, reminding me that if I was given the position I should never forget that honouring Bruce's memory would always be in the forefront. Bruce is never far from my mind on any given day, so agreeing with that was not a problem.

It was easy to say that I'd apply, but when the time came, I had second thoughts—not about whether I wanted to become the next national president, but if I would be the best choice for MADD Canada. The questions kept circling in my mind. *Should I? Could I? Yes? No! Maybe…* I had almost decided not to apply when I heard a little voice over my shoulder. "If you don't try, you will always wonder if you could have made it. You're just afraid." My son was sending me back my own words, spoken to him so long ago, and he was right. I was afraid.

There is no doubt in my mind that Bruce stood over me as I wrote my presentation for the selection committee. I worked for weeks making it look as professional as possible. I wanted to pay tribute to Bruce and all the victims of impaired driving. Those victims on the memorial wall spoke to me, and needed someone to speak for them. I put everything into my application and knew that if it wasn't successful, I had at least tried my best.

Then I had to deal with my quest on a more personal level—I went shopping for a suit that wouldn't show the effects of travel. I was flying from Halifax to Toronto and going directly to the interview, and I wanted to look professional so that the selection committee would know I was serious about the position. After a day of shopping I was ready to go.

Robert dropped me off at the airport in Halifax that morning with a quick kiss and wishes of good luck. I was feeling good about my presentation and the professional clothes, but that didn't stop the jitters. I made a quick stop to the restroom before the flight to make sure my hair and makeup were satisfactory. I knew that once I arrived in Toronto there would be no time to look myself over, and I was more nervous than I'd ever been. As I turned away from the mirror, I noticed something hanging. The price tags under my arm were dangling for all to see. Oh my! It was a Minnie Pearl moment that had me laughing, and reminded me not to take myself so seriously. I resolved to have a good time with the interview and enjoy the experience.

It was the first time I had been to the national headquarters of MADD Canada, and I was surprised. The offices weren't elaborate or fancy, just functional. And not a bit of space was unused. Most striking was the official memorial wall (I'd seen a more compact, travelling version at the conference). I knew that it was at our national office but had never realized the extent, the sheer magnitude of the wall—which in fact wasn't just one wall but almost every wall. All the photos were framed identically and given the same degree of importance. Crash dates ranged from the 1950s to the present. The impact was staggering. I felt the weight of responsibility to these victims as I passed by. I was getting choked up. I hadn't seen Bruce's photo yet and knew that when I did, it would be my undoing. I walked into the interview room and was warmly welcomed by the committee members, all smiling, enjoying their morning coffee. They had several interviews that day and mine was the first.

The interview was an intense two-hour process made a pleasure by the receptive faces at the table. At first I was nervous, but a single thought of my Minnie Pearl moment put it all into perspective. I relaxed, had fun, and left with the knowledge that I had fulfilled my goal by doing my best. Bruce would have been proud. Now it was up to MADD Canada.

CHAPTER 5

Honouring Our Son

In the late fall of 2006, I was finally given the opportunity to thank police officers for the support they gave our family after Bruce's death. I often thought of their generous actions, so when they asked if I would speak at Operation Christmas as the mother of a police officer who had been killed by impaired driving, I readily agreed. Operation Christmas is a program that brings Nova Scotian municipal police, RCMP, paramedics, military police, and other stakeholders together to do sobriety road checks and promote safe and sober driving over the holiday season. I was going to tell Bruce's story at the launch, a formal banquet. And I would finally get the chance to say thank you to all those wonderful men and women who filled the funeral home and lined the streets of our village in honour of Bruce.

I spent an agonizing week planning how to tell them more about Bruce and his hopes and dreams. I wanted them to know how much their support meant to us as a family. I also wanted to tell them about MADD Canada and how much our missions are intertwined. My speech was tough to write and I was afraid that I wouldn't be able to get the words out—that I would break down and not be able to correctly portray the depth of my gratitude for the policing family.

On the day of the banquet, I shook as I took my place behind the podium. There were two hundred or more in the audience. I began by thanking them for the opportunity to speak and told them about MADD Canada. I told them that MADD Canada is a grassroots organization made up of parents, police, paramedics, community leaders, and other citizens, all with the common goal of eliminating impaired driving and the killing and maiming it causes. The MADD mission statement is to "stop impaired driving and support victims of this violent crime." That is a powerful goal, but is it realistic? I believe it is, and I told the audience that we work on it every day.

I told them that a balanced program of public awareness, education, legislation, and aggressive enforcement by police, crown attorneys, and the courts is essential to eliminating impaired driving. That while an individual's right to consume alcohol is a private matter, driving after drinking is a public matter. MADD Canada believes that impaired drivers must be held accountable for their behaviour and that Canadians must understand that driving is a privilege, not a right as so many believe.

I told them about MADD Canada's wish list, well researched and proven to be effective. At that point, our goal was to see every province adopt these initiatives:

- a zero percent blood alcohol count (BAC) to age twenty-one in the graduated license program;
- increased police enforcement powers, giving officers the power to demand documentation and establish sobriety checkpoints, as well as the authority to demand standard field sobriety tests and samples from drivers in fatal or personal injury crashes;
- short-term administrative suspensions when a driver registers more than a 0.05 percent BAC;
- an effective, mandatory alcohol interlock program in all provinces (that means that all drivers convicted of driving impaired would have

the interlock device installed in their vehicles to ensure that these vehicles could not be operated when the driver is impaired); and
- a vehicle impoundment or forfeiture program for those who choose to drive repeatedly without a license.

Many of these measures are now in place and we know that lives have been saved as a result. In fact, in the last twenty years MADD Canada programs are believed to have saved over twenty thousand lives in Canada.

I gave my audience at the Operation Christmas launch some more disturbing statistics—that every day in Canada four people die as a result of impaired driving, and another two hundred are injured. That translates to almost seventy thousand people injured or killed each year in Canada alone. I reminded them that impaired driving is still the leading criminal cause of death in our country.

The speech became harder when I had to get more personal. I said, "But you know all this! Many of you are the first responders. You see the carnage, the tears, and tragedy. You see the terrible waste of human life again and again. Some of you will have to go to that door and see the eyes of the mom or dad as you tell them that their child or loved one won't be coming home ever again. And the big question is, why?"

And then I told them about Bruce.

"If he was here, he'd be standing over there…all 6'3" and 240 pounds of him. Noticeable even in this room! His arms would be crossed in front of him and he'd have a big grin on his face. He probably would be sitting next to the prettiest girl in the room. If you had a chance to shake his hand or give him a hug you would have felt his quiet strength. But he's not here today, because of an impaired driver."

I told them how Bruce became a police officer and how much he loved his career. I shared the Bruce I knew and loved and in the end they got to know him and appreciate how much we all had lost.

Bruce was alive in the room that night.

I shared with them the night that forever changed our lives, getting the call and all the horrors that followed.

Finally, I had the opportunity to say thank you:

I pay tribute to all of you…for I learned something. Bruce's family didn't end at the four walls of our home—nor at the borders of our community, nor even Nova Scotia. That wonderful policing family extended across the country, giving us support every step of the way. Bruce didn't have brothers at home, but in policing he had brothers and sisters everywhere. Your support at the hospital, at the funeral, at the memorial in Springhill, and even later at home showed our family the depth of your commitment to a fellow officer, your brother, our son.

Now it is my turn to help. By sharing Bruce's story with you, I hope to help you in the battle against impaired driving. All it will take is one person who decides not to drive impaired to make a difference. One person at a time.

If you have ever wondered if it's worth it, if you have ever grown weary or felt you were getting a little jaded or bitter, if you ever close your eyes at night and have flashbacks of that last horrible crash scene—that child or teenager in your arms, if you've ever felt frustrated that you can't stop impaired driving, or hear someone's lawyer make a statement like "Why bother? You'll never stop drunk driving," think again. Remember Bruce.

We will stop impaired driving together. Maybe not today or tomorrow, but it's coming—new legislation, more awareness, and better tools for you to do your job to the best of your ability. One person at a time, one more checkpoint, one more impaired driver off the road, one more family celebrating Christmas this year instead of mourning a child lost.

Thank you…together we can make a difference.

There, I did it! My nervousness disappeared and I released a huge sigh of relief as I left the podium. The officers and officials all stood, applauding as I took my seat.

Thank you, Bruce, for helping me through this, was my silent prayer. Later in the evening, several officers came over to me to express their gratitude for what MADD is doing and many shared that they too, had been at Bruce's funeral or memorial service. It was a good night.

After that I found myself speaking to large groups more and more, sharing my son with people and letting his death influence whenever possible. My grief had evolved. I still missed Bruce terribly but now felt that instead of absorbing all the pain I could turn it around and make it something more. Bruce could still carry on his mission to serve and protect, through me.

Meanwhile I was still waiting to hear the results from my interview. I can't say that I *calmly* waited. I'm a person who wants results yesterday, so waiting was tough and I kept replaying the interview in my head, thinking of ways I could have made improvements.

My friend's husband, Doug, commented about all the important people I'd get to meet if I got the position. My answer was simply: "The important people are the ones here at home. The powerful people I may meet are the ones who can make change."

I still stand by that comment. I've never met anyone who could compare to my husband, daughters, and friends, and the love and support they give me. They are my rocks, the most important people in my life.

The phone call I was waiting for came in February. Carolyn Swinson, chair of the national board of MADD Canada, told me that my interview had been outstanding and they would be pleased to have me serve as national president.

She told me that a press release would go out later in the week and I should expect many calls. Carolyn was right, and I felt more than a little awkward with all the attention. The person who was once terrified at the thought of media had become the spokesperson for MADD Canada. Still, with the training provided by MADD Canada and the support of the national staff, I soon became able to deal with the press more easily, sometimes even on a daily basis.

One thing eases the stress of talking to the media on behalf of MADD: We are right. Our research comes from the most impeccable sources and our recommendations come from studies of legislation in other countries where they have been much more successful in decreasing the deaths and injuries on their roads due to impaired driving. Sadly, Canada is behind in legislative change and so much more should and could easily be done. Reaching out to the politicians who can make change and encouraging them to do the right thing is a top priority.

Therefore one of the first things I was asked to do, even before I officially became national president, was sit in on appointments that the national office had set up with MPs in Ottawa. The current president, Karen Dunham, was there, as well as our CEO, Andrew Murie, and director of legal policy, Robert Solomon. It was a busy two days of meetings, getting to know these folks and making contact with legislators on behalf of MADD Canada. The last meeting of the visit was with our Minister of Justice, Hon. Rob Nicholson.

I knew that this meeting was regarded as the highlight of our visit and I was a little apprehensive about meeting the minister. Minister Nicholson came into the boardroom and welcomed us all warmly and spoke of his own experience as a lawyer dealing with impaired drivers. We thanked him for the meeting and I told him a little about Bruce and why I was involved with MADD Canada.

He paid close attention and really seemed to relate on a personal level to my family's loss. I was impressed, and we left the meeting with hopes for great change. In the years that followed we were not disappointed as Minister Nicholson called for legislation to make that change. There is no doubt in my mind that he has helped to ensure that impaired drivers pay for their crimes, and more importantly his legislative reforms serve as a preventative measure to save lives. On Bruce's birthday in 2007, I stood with the minister as he introduced legislation that would close the legal loopholes that allowed impaired drivers to escape criminal convictions and walk free.

His bill also addressed drug-impaired driving, a milestone for both MADD Canada and police forces across Canada. It gave them the necessary power to be able to charge and convict drug-impaired drivers like never before.

It was tough being away from my family on Bruce's birthday. It's a day we always spend together, but on that day Bruce was with me.

It was my honour to have the opportunity to present to Minister Nicholson MADD Canada's 2009 Citizen of Distinction Award at our national leadership conference for the work he has done to stop impaired driving. He has saved Canadian lives.

As the voice of the members and victims of MADD Canada, it was not uncommon for me to be asked for interviews on almost a daily basis. I had to be well informed all the time, and it was up to me to make sure I had all the facts going into any situation. The national office was great at making sure that I was comfortable with any media situation. One tip that I often remembered was that it's not about answering the question but about delivering the message. Another is that we never forget the victims. Our work is all about stopping the loss of human life.

I remember one particular radio talk show where listeners could actually call in and talk to me. I really loved this kind of show, because I never knew what was coming around the bend. I found it fun to dispute an issue when I had all the facts and figures to prove I was in the right. One gentleman came on the air and he was furious. He called MADD Canada a bunch of zealots with their own agenda and added that we were all busy filling our pockets at the donors' expense. I actually started to laugh. His accusations were ridiculous. I told him that yes, indeed, we did have an agenda. It was to stop the senseless waste of life on our highways and to continue to support the victims of impaired driving. As for where donated money goes, I let him know that MADD Canada is completely in compliance with the Canada Revenue Agency and our financials are available on our website for anyone to see. As to filling our pockets—well, as national president, even I was a volunteer!

Another day I was talking about Campaign 911 on a local radio show. This is a MADD Canada campaign that encourages all citizens to call 911 and report anyone who they suspect is driving impaired. One gentleman called in to say that he was sick of all the "rat lines." I countered by saying that citizens call 911 because they want to get impaired drivers off the road. These callers are our heroes and have made it their own personal mission to make our roads safer. They have saved many people from becoming victims—maybe even that angry man's loved ones.

Other interviews were much more serious—like those held after a repeat offender killed someone while driving impaired, or when someone walked away from a charge on a technicality. Those were the tough interviews, when I had to think about what a long way we still had to go.

Quite often we would meet with provincial governments to make recommendations about their impaired driving legislation. It was great to see so many of the provinces bringing our recommendations into law. The Rating the Provinces (RTP) report, an ongoing study that reviews and evaluates each jurisdiction's impaired driving legislation, lets all the provinces and territories see where they rate in the country in their legislative reform. Just like in school, everyone wants to earn an A—and the great part is that each A means lives have been saved. These meetings with provincial governments were satisfying, since it felt like they led to real change. For example, the 2006 RTP report had Nova Scotia ranked eleventh for its impaired driving legislation. That placing didn't sit well with local government and they were very supportive of making the changes that were proven to save the lives of Nova Scotians. It certainly was my pleasure to let officials know that in the 2009 report, Nova Scotia had moved up to fourth place in Canada, after Ontario, Manitoba, and Prince Edward Island. It was a good day for Canada.

Much of my time was also devoted to thanking donors for their support. I loved calling all around the country to thank people for helping MADD. Sometimes I'd get a hesitant "Thank you for calling…now, don't you want more?" I'd say no, that I was just calling to say thank you. Donors were surprised. Once in a while I'd ask why someone had chosen to support MADD. One young woman laughed and said that her husband had been caught driving impaired and she was going to make sure he paid for it the rest of his life! I shared that one with the national board and they loved it.

Some people would tell me about their communities and how rampant impaired driving was there, and that donating was their way of doing something to fight against it. Yet another young woman told me that she had seen the multimedia show at her school years before and felt that it had changed her life, and now she was paying it forward.

Sometimes, I would hear that someone had donated because they had lost a loved one or been hurt themselves. That opened the door to providing them with victim support. After a long chat I always asked if I could forward their information to Gloria.

My days were full, as were many of my evenings. I was happier than I had been since Bruce's death.

❋ ❋ ❋

All during this time I relied on Susan MacAskill, the Atlantic Region Chapter Services manager. Susan is a patient woman with a calm manner who easily resolves the many problems that can crop up in a large organization. She served as national president ten years before me, and she was a wonderful mentor to me during my own tenure. She had lost her father, Donald King, to a drunk driver. Her story was the first victim story I ever heard, and it affected me on the deepest level. I had never taken the opportunity to ask for more of the details—the things she might not have told the audience I was part of when I heard her story the first time.

Susan and I took a lot of long drives—it wasn't unusual for us to drive to an event even five hours away in support of a chapter or for a special function. But our conversations always made the drives go by quickly. We usually talked primarily about chapter issues, but one day in 2009, I asked Susan to tell me more about the crash that claimed her father's life and brought her to MADD Canada.

Susan's loss wasn't as sudden as others', but instead took place over the hardest ten days of her life. Just retelling the story was tough on her.

It was a Friday evening in late August 1993. Susan was finishing the last week of a vacation, and remembered wishing she could have just a few more days. She and her husband, Archie, had enjoyed a wonderful day on the South Shore, picnicking and sightseeing in beautiful Mahone Bay and Chester.

They debated going to the dinner theatre at the Chester Playhouse, but for some reason decided against it and headed for home. During the drive, they talked about the summer coming to an end. Archie's father had died just two months earlier, and Archie and Susan were just starting to process the loss of another parent to a terminal illness. It had only been two years since Susan's mother had died of cancer, and they felt like they had relived so many of the same experiences.

It seemed like it had been so long since they had had a normal lifestyle—much of the past three and a half years had been devoted to taking care of their parents. But in spite of everything, they still agreed that things were good. Because of all of that had happened in the previous months, they were probably especially aware of how fragile and precious life really is.

They had only been home in Windsor about an hour when the phone rang. It was Susan's brother, Paul.

Susan says that she'll never forget the urgency in his voice—when she answered, she could hear him saying, "Come on, pick up, pick up…"

She asked her brother what was wrong. He answered that it was their father and stepmother, Dorothy. Their father was being transported to Halifax by ambulance. Paul told her he'd be there to pick her up in ten minutes.

Susan was standing in her driveway when Paul and his wife, Shelley, arrived. She jumped into their van and they were on their way in seconds. Their sister Andrea's house was their next stop. Once she was on board they hit the highway for Halifax.

Paul knew very few details. Dorothy had called him from the emergency department at Colchester Regional Hospital in Truro. They had been involved in a car crash just outside of Truro. Dorothy was being treated for a broken arm and collarbone, but she said that her husband was unconscious and needed immediate surgery. She told Paul that he and his siblings needed to get to the Victoria General Hospital in Halifax right away. The mere fact that he was being sent there rather than being treated in Truro indicated that his injuries were very serious. Dorothy was right to be worried.

Nobody in that van remembers much about the drive that night. They just couldn't get to Halifax fast enough.

Susan and her family were ushered into a waiting room and were surprised to find that they had actually arrived ahead of the ambulance coming in from Truro. They watched as the paramedics wheeled their father in on the stretcher.

Susan recognized Jeff, one of the paramedics, and saw the pained look on his face. Then, finally, she saw her dad. That's when her whole horrible nightmare began to feel much more real. It was such a shock for the family to see someone they loved so helpless, so injured, and so lifeless. Susan says that she'll never forget what she saw that night.

She and her family waited at the hospital all night while their father was in surgery. The doctors needed to stop his internal bleeding and set his broken bones. Several times during the night a nurse gave them an update and explained what was going on in the hope that the news would put their minds at ease. By this time Susan's other sisters, Heather and Carol, had arrived.

The solemn group sat through the night speculating as to what might have happened to cause the accident. Was it a heart attack? A blown tire?

Eventually they found out that their father and Dorothy had been driving home when they were hit by another car. The driver of the other vehicle was in critical condition and undergoing surgery as well. Police said they had reason to believe that the other driver might have been drinking.

Susan says that's when everything changed for her.

Up until that point they had been looking for some logical explanation for what had caused the accident, and the possibility that it was an error on their father's part. To discover that it was someone else's bad decision was sickening.

Dawn broke on Saturday morning, and they had been up all night, still waiting to hear the results of the surgery.

Susan and her siblings began to make phone calls to tell family and friends what was happening—that their dad had been in surgery all night, that he was still in surgery, and that they weren't optimistic about his prospects. After the first twenty-four hours, however, they became more hopeful—they felt it was a good sign that he had made it that far, and they tentatively began to voice their optimism.

Finally, on Sunday afternoon they were allowed into the intensive care unit to see their father. It was a much different picture than when he had been brought in on the stretcher Friday night. He was completely covered in clean, white bandages, and his left leg was in traction. It was upsetting to see his skin discoloured from the damage to his liver, but more shocking was his swollen body. He looked like a sumo wrestler. They were asked to leave after only ten minutes.

On Monday Susan and her siblings had to go back to work. They decided to take alternate days off so that someone would always be with their father. Those days were difficult for Susan—the challenge of keeping up with things at home, parenting teenagers, preparing meals, working full-time, and the daily trips to Halifax, an hour away.

There was no positive news from hospital staff on her father's condition. Though some of the lacerations on his arms began to heal, and the surgery had successfully stopped internal bleeding and set the broken bones, their father had not regained consciousness. Apparently his head had been forced into the windshield of his car, and doctors were concerned at the level of brain damage he may have incurred, so he was transferred to neurological intensive care for testing.

On Thursday evening Susan and Carol were at their father's side when two doctors asked if they could speak with them about the results of those tests.

They went into great detail about the tests, including how the different parts of the brain should respond to testing. Their father's brain had not responded to any of the tests.

During this summary, Susan began to dread what would come next. In a desperate attempt to keep from hearing the question she knew she was going to hear, Susan tried to take charge of the situation. She remembers saying, "Just a minute, you don't know my dad."

She wanted them to know who they were about to give up on. She wanted to change their minds. So she told them about her dad, Donald King. She told them about his life and the values he had instilled in her and her siblings: to strive to overcome their limitations, to always show consideration and respect for others, to make the right choices, and to make the most of their opportunities. She told them that when he regained consciousness he would do whatever it took to rehabilitate himself.

Susan remembers the doctors' faces as she finished her plea and when she was finally done, they repeated themselves—her father's brain had not responded to their tests, which meant he would never regain consciousness.

Then they posed the question that Susan had been dreading. They asked for permission to remove Donald's life support.

Susan says she asked the stupidest question of her life then. She asked the doctors what would happen if they were wrong. What if this was the one-in-a-million case, and they never found out because they removed his life support? She asked if they believed in miracles, and told them that she did.

They began again: "We're very sorry, but there's no possible way…"

Susan and Carol knew that they couldn't give an answer that night. They had their other siblings and their stepmother to consult. Over the course of the next two days they gathered as a family to consider the doctors' request.

Susan was only thirty-eight years old at the time, and it remains the toughest decision she has ever had to make.

They spent two days reflecting on all the valuable things their parents had taught them, on how their mother's long illness had allowed them the time to fulfill many of her last wishes, and they knew they wanted to be able to do the same for their father.

The family knew that they all had to be in agreement with their decision and if even one of them couldn't live in peace with the decision to remove life support, then they wouldn't.

It was their oldest sister, Andrea, who reminded them of a day they had spent with their parents several years earlier. On that afternoon their mother reminded her children that they would be spending their winters in Florida, and would be driving.

She said if she were ever critically injured in an accident, she did not want to be sustained by life support. Their father had agreed that that would be his wish also.

When Andrea reminded them of what their parents had said that day seven years earlier, she added that they could actually grant their father his last wish.

It was a quiet sunny Sunday afternoon when the life support was turned off. It had been nine days since their whole nightmare had begun.

Overnight, their father's lungs began to fill up with fluid. Susan remembers him struggling to breathe. I can't imagine how hard it was for her and her family. At 4:03 p.m. on Monday, September 6, her father, the man who had given her life and made her the person she is, breathed his last breath. Donald King's battle for life was over.

Susan was standing by her father's bed with her husband, Carol, and Dorothy in those final moments. They were invited to take as long as they needed.

Susan remembers walking out of the hospital into the early evening air. The sun was setting. Her eyes filled with tears. Her world had been ripped apart.

Several days after the funeral, Susan and Carol met with an officer from the Bible Hill RCMP to see what would happen regarding criminal proceedings. They knew that the man responsible for their father's death had been drinking that night and that he had survived his surgery. The sisters were adamant that there be charges laid and a day in court for their family.

The officer went over the file with them, indicating that there were witnesses willing to testify to what they had seen that night. She also told Susan and Carol that there was evidence of the driver's alcohol use, including a receipt from a liquor store in Truro dated the day of the crash.

The RCMP laid several charges: impaired driving causing death, impaired driving causing bodily harm, dangerous driving causing death, dangerous driving causing bodily harm, and numerous violations of the motor vehicle act for operating a car while suspended from driving, without vehicle registration or insurance.

Susan and Carol could see that the officer had all her paperwork in order, but nothing could have prepared Susan for what she saw next. Among the file papers was her father's autopsy report from the hospital. As she began to read through it, Susan became aware of the extent of her father's injuries and the internal damage that had been caused by the crash. But seeing the cause of death was the hardest part for her to read.

On that line was one word: *Pneumonia*. That's it.

It didn't matter that a drunk driver had caused the crash. The doctors had deemed that Donald King died because his lungs filled up. He had pneumonia.

"No, no, no," she said, determined that this was not the way it would end. She was determined that this story, the truth, would be told.

That November, the driver entered a plea of not guilty at the first court appearance. Then there was plea-bargaining—in exchange for the driver's guilty plea, the charges of impaired driving causing death and impaired driving causing bodily harm were dropped.

In April 1994, thirty-eight-year-old Lawrence Vincent Works of Truro Heights was sentenced to three and a half years in prison for dangerous driving causing death, a concurrent two-year sentence for dangerous driving causing bodily harm, and an eight-year driving prohibition.

The King family was deeply unsatisfied with this outcome. The length of Works's prison sentence was not an appropriate exchange for killing their father, but unfortunately the legal system isn't about settling the score. Sometimes it's about compromise.

In August 1995, Susan requested permission from Westmorland Institute, a minimum-security facility in Dorchester, New Brunswick, to attend any of Works's parole hearings. She wanted a chance to speak face-to-face with the man who had taken her father's life and let him know the pain he had caused their family, especially since she and her family had not been permitted to deliver victim impact statements during the court proceedings.

But she received a deeply dismaying answer from the penitentiary. Works had been paroled in December 1994. He served just seven months of a three-and-a-half-year sentence. The King family had not been notified of any of his parole proceedings.

Susan's frustration at this point made her turn a corner. She felt that no consideration had been given to her and her family. She asked herself, "Who *does* anything about this?"

That's when she turned to MADD Canada—for help, support, and answers to some of her questions. She found out that the nearest chapter was in Happy Valley-Goose Bay, Labrador.

That chapter was clearly too far away for her to join, so she decided to start a chapter in the Windsor–Annapolis Valley area. She applied to MADD Canada's national office, and representatives came to Nova Scotia and hosted a town hall meeting to determine whether there was enough interest in Susan's community to maintain a MADD chapter—it takes a board of five people to start a chapter.

MADD Canada was pleased to issue the Annapolis Valley chapter charter status a few months later. It was the nineteenth chapter in Canada. MADD Canada helped to train chapter members by giving them the materials they needed, and of course they were always only a phone call away. They also brought the Annapolis Valley volunteers to Toronto to join other volunteers from across Canada at training sessions.

Founding members are encouraged to involve the public in the battle against drunk driving, and soon members were partnering with police and handing out MADD's trademark red ribbons. They did mall displays and took part in local parades. They became listed in the local phone directory and soon received calls from other victims in the area. They were able to support these victims and help them to pay tribute to their loved ones or acknowledge their own injuries.

For Susan, this was still not enough, and a short while later she was asked to represent MADD Canada as its national president. She served a two-year term and helped start MADD chapters all over Canada. She became the person who "does something about this." She became someone who would fight to right the wrongs.

Fifteen years later, she is still righting the wrongs and striving to make a difference. Still working as a staff member for MADD Canada as the chapter services manager for the Atlantic region, as she was the day she told me the story about losing her father to drunk driving, Susan has helped to start twenty-seven chapters and has helped eight community leaders (another role volunteers can play with MADD) as they make a difference in their communities.

MADD Canada went from having one chapter in the Atlantic provinces to being an authoritative voice on impaired driving.

Susan has saved lives. Is there any question? And when we thank her for her hard work and involvement, she talks about others who have influenced her, the wonderful people she has met. Some have experienced a personal loss, like her. Many others have not, but still want to help and give of themselves.

Susan has had many opportunities to share her personal story and influence others. Every day, she is reminded of how uncertain life is, and she is grateful for the valuable lessons her father taught her and his passion for life. She remembers how he lived life to the fullest and how he was able to laugh at himself.

Her father was confident in his strengths and vulnerable in his weaknesses. Even though his untimely death has had a tragic impact on Susan, she is fulfilled in knowing that he still has such a profound influence on her life.

Although I never knew Donald King, his life, the man he was, and his death have affected me and countless others, in particular those of us in Atlantic Canada. He brought us Susan, and he brought us MADD Canada. And what has MADD brought this little bit of Canada? It has helped to create change in a culture where drinking and driving was historically commonplace and considered a rite of passage.

Every day brings new challenges for Susan, both personally and in her work with MADD Canada. It is very clear to her why she does what she does.

She does it to honour her dad.

CHAPTER 6

A Mother's Tears

I love Facebook; it lets me connect with people. Some I don't know well but are involved with MADD Canada. Some are volunteers, some victims, but all have become my friends. We share tragedy and triumph. The good days and the bad.

One day I received a friend request from a woman named Desma—an unusual name that sounded a little familiar, though I couldn't put a face to it. I accepted her request nonetheless. Her status updates were so filled with pain and anguish my heart ached for her. She would write of how she missed her son beyond belief and wanted to join him. I became truly alarmed for this woman and kept watching for more. Many days she would send messages to her son, Matthew, letting him know how much she loved him, and post pictures of happier days gone by. Her words touched my heart; they reflected the pain I had once known. Sometimes I would respond, trying to give her the tiniest bit of relief from her grieving.

A few months later MADD Canada had meetings arranged in St. John's and I was asked to attend. We were meeting with Minister O'Brien about legislative changes that would benefit Newfoundland and Labrador, and with Royal Newfoundland Constabulary Chief Brown to talk about the Campaign 911 program—its success in other areas and its introduction in Newfoundland and Labrador.

To celebrate a successful day of meetings, the MADD Avalon chapter president, Christine Care, invited us to a potluck at her adorable home on a quaint side street in St John's. She welcomed me into her kitchen and I spent an hour or so with her as she prepared a traditional Newfoundland dish called fish and brewis. It's made of salt fish and hard tack. I'm not a seafood lover, but when in Rome—or should I say, when in St. John's...

Christine is an amazing volunteer who lost her mother many years ago to an impaired driver. She works to make change in her province every day, and the best way I could ever describe her is as a firecracker. She is committed, enthusiastic, and very vocal. I was looking forward to meeting more of the chapter members and was thrilled to finally meet Desma. It turned out that we had met at the most recent victims' weekend for a few moments, which explains why I remembered her name—and I was pleased I could now place it with her face.

Seeing Desma was shocking. She looked like someone who had been through a war. The pain was visible in her eyes and in all her movements. My heart ached for her.

We sat on a stool in Christine's kitchen as she told me a little of what had happened to Matthew. Her story held me both spellbound and outraged for the next hour or more. Matthew was killed on March 28, 2005—Easter Monday.

I wish I could say that I couldn't imagine what she had gone through; the trouble is, I *can* imagine. The details are different, but we share the same pain.

Rod and Desma Churchill were a typical Newfoundland couple. They were wonderful parents and should have had a house full of children, but medical problems prevented that from happening. Their only son,

Matthew, was himself a miracle and they poured all their love and hope for the future into him. He didn't disappoint them. At fifteen, Matthew was a son to be proud of. He was blond, beautiful, and best of all, had a good and generous heart. He was involved in everything imaginable and was wildly popular in school.

Matthew was always helping out those less fortunate and Desma told me that sometimes he would come home from school actually missing clothing. Someone might have needed something and Matthew knew that he could share. Other nights he'd come home starving because he had loaned someone his lunch money.

Rod was the local minor hockey coach and Desma was very happy in her job and also in her most important role, as Matthew's mom. Matthew was the shining star in their world, and their lives revolved around him. Theirs was the home that many of Matthew's friends called their second home. It was a safe place to hang out.

The boys used to spend a lot of their time practicing for their newly formed band. Matthew played the guitar as he did everything, with passion. They called the band "Zero Tolerance," something that later would seem so prophetic.

It was an evening like any other in their Portugal Cove home. Desma had gotten home a little earlier after picking up Matthew and his friend Greg from Greg's house. The boys had been playing hockey and now Desma was in the kitchen making the hungry two-some some supper. Soon after supper the boys decided that they were going to meet some friends just up the road. They were going to walk, even though Desma strongly objected because she was nervous of dangerous or inattentive drivers. She tried to convince them to wait for Rod to get home from the rink so he could take them, but Matthew and Greg couldn't be persuaded and started to pull on their jackets. Desma offered to drive the boys herself, but Matthew just said, "Don't be so foolish, Mom."

"It's not you I'm worried about," she replied. "It's the other drivers I don't trust."

They convinced Desma that they would be all right, but Desma's last words to her son were "I can only hope that one day when you have children of your own, you will understand."

The boys left and ten minutes later the phone rang.

Desma answered at once, and heard, "Mrs. Churchill, this is Brendan, come quick; Matthew has been hit by a car!"

She dropped the phone and screamed for her father, who lived downstairs. The two ran for the car with their minds going in every direction. Run, walk, drive, hurry. Desma just had to get to Matthew… and quickly!

She sat in the car while every possible scenario crossed her mind and she could only hope that she was overreacting, that she would just find him a little bruised.

She pushed her father to hurry and he replied "Oh Jesus, I left the keys in the house."

Desma felt the strength just drain from her body as she waited. She had never in her life felt more hopeless or desolate. All she could think of was her baby lying by the road, bleeding and in pain without her being there for him. She jumped out of the car and began running. Her father finally caught up with her and made her get in. Almost immediately the pair could see the lights and hear the sirens of emergency vehicles.

Desma realized how serious the accident must be and began to feel sick. They drove until they were forcibly blocked; then she jumped out of the car before it came to a full stop. The scene before her was surreal. It seemed like a haze was hanging over everything. Then she saw Matthew's friends Brandon and Gregory sitting on a large red box, and asked them where Matthew was.

Brandon pointed toward the ditch just up the road.

Desma tried to get closer but felt the arms of the firefighters holding her back. She pleaded with them and asked why they were stopping her. She told them that she just wanted to sit there beside her son and hold him. She promised not to hurt anything and told them that she wanted to kiss him and hold him and let him know that his mom was there.

Desma says that she kept calling out Matthew's name and still they held her back. She hoped to hear his voice answering, "Mom, I'm over here." It didn't happen.

Not being able to touch her son or be with him is probably the thing that will always upset Desma the most. She was Matthew's mother and she deserved and needed to be with him.

Desma picked up her phone and called Rod for help. When he answered, she screamed that Matthew had been hit by a car. Rod had been tied up in the traffic on the other side of the crash scene, not knowing that his son was involved. He abandoned his car and ran toward the flashing lights.

He, too, was stopped by firefighters and police. He felt helpless as he begged and pleaded with the officials to let him get through. He needed to hold his wife in his arms and once even thought he could hear her voice as she called out to their son. Tears streamed down his cheeks as he begged to be allowed to get closer but still he was refused.

He watched helplessly as they performed CPR on Matthew and thought back to earlier in the day, the last time he'd seen his son. Rod fell to his knees sobbing, trying to remember the last words that were said out loud. He wondered if he'd even said goodbye. He watched from one side of the crash scene while Desma watched from the other, neither able to reach the other or their treasured son.

Desma continued to call for Matthew as he was loaded into the ambulance and she was filled with anger toward those who were stopping her from reaching him. She saw Gregory get into the ambulance with Matthew and questioned why—why him and not her. She was Matthew's mother and he needed her! She begged to be allowed to go into the ambulance.

Desma didn't realize that Greg was in shock and had been hit by Matthew's body as it was thrown through the air, and needed medical attention himself. Later, Greg proved to be a valuable witness; he had seen the driver fleeing from the scene after the hit-and-run.

As paramedics closed the ambulance doors, Desma finally saw Rod and he, her. Desma ran and put her arms around him, closing her eyes and hoping that when she opened them Matthew would be in her bedroom, shaking her awake. That it would all have been a nightmare. But it wasn't. Every parent's worst nightmare had come true for them that night.

Together they sat in their car, holding each other, following the ambulance to the hospital. Others in the car said the words, voiced the hope that he was young and strong and would make it. But Rod knew in his heart what Desma had yet to learn. Their Matthew was gone.

Shortly after they arrived at the hospital, a Dr. Hatcher came to see them. The doctor told Desma and Rod that Matthew had been seriously hurt but that they were doing everything they could. Soon she came back again and told them they were inserting a breathing tube into Matthew. The third time she came into the waiting room, tears covered her face. Despite all their efforts, Matthew had not survived.

Desma fell to the floor and Rod stood rigid in shock. Their world had just ceased to exist. The pain was unbearable, indescribable, unrelenting, worse than anything they could have imagined. After a short while, Rod asked to see his son.

Unbelievably, after everything else that had happened, the injustices were just beginning. Matthew's body had become evidence, and Rod could do no more than look at him, sit in a nearby chair, and touch his leg. How he must have longed to hold his son, to touch his face, to make everything all right. But he couldn't. After a time Rod was able to leave Matthew to the police and the coroner, so they could do their work. Desma couldn't bring herself to see Matthew's body.

She didn't see him at the hospital or at the funeral home. The last time she saw her son he was smiling and telling her not to worry as he left her side and walked into the arms of God.

After a time they returned to their home and the certainty of having to face a life without their son, a life that Desma no longer wanted to live. Although their community supported the couple far more than Desma ever would have expected, the weight of her grief soon took a toll on her health, and she was rushed to hospital suffering a severe anxiety attack. The couple started meeting with a psychologist. The process of grief counselling had begun.

How can someone tell you how to stop missing your child? How can someone give you hope when your future is gone? A long desolate road loomed ahead for the Churchills.

Meanwhile, the RNC was also doing their job, searching for the hit-and-run driver. They had finally found the car; the registration information led them to the owner, who refused to give police information about who was driving at the time of the crash. Meanwhile the community was outraged and filled with disbelief that someone in Portugal Cove could leave a young boy's broken and damaged body on the side of the road without a glance in his rearview mirror. What monster lived in their town?

It wasn't long before they had the answer. After a stay at a nearby hotel, Robert Parsons—not the owner of the car, but the driver—turned himself in to the police.

I don't dwell on the drivers who have been responsible for many of the stories in this book and mostly have not mentioned names. The only reason I've mentioned Robert Parsons is because the trauma of Matthew's death was compounded by Mr. Parson's actions. Apparently the driver had been at a friend's house, where he had several drinks.

He got behind the wheel to go home, and he somehow doesn't remember hitting Matthew just moments later. In court he remembered everything about his activities that night, but somehow forgot that one small, fatal incident. How convenient. On the advice of his lawyer he left his home the night of the crash and checked into a nearby motel, not turning himself in to the police for three days. This made it impossible to prove that he was impaired at the time of the crash, and Mr. Parsons was never convicted of any alcohol-related crime.

The gruelling sixteen-month trial only extended the grief felt by the Churchill family and Matthew's friends. Finally, Mr. Parsons was found guilty of failing to remain at the scene of an accident. The only solace for Rod comes from knowing that the offender now has to spend the rest of his life with the general public of Newfoundland knowing that he's the person who killed Matthew Churchill and tried to hide his crime.

Meanwhile, Rod and Desma are left to try to make some sense of their lives without Matthew.

I asked Desma how she came to MADD Canada and she told me that her first contact with the organization was in high school. She had heard some victim stories and felt the pain of those victims. Never did she think that MADD would someday play such a big part in her life, or that MADD would be helping her on her own life's journey.

A few weeks after Matthew was killed, she came upon a package with information about MADD Canada in it. Slowly, she began to read through all the literature and quickly discovered that she and Rod were not alone.

She realized that there were many other victims like them. Desma was shocked.

Soon she called and spoke on the phone with Gloria Appleby, the same woman who had answered my call for help just a year before. She said that Gloria always listened to her babbling, ranting, and even the silence when no words would come out for the tears and the sadness in her throat.

Gloria would end all of their conversations with the offer that Desma could call her any time. She had also become Desma's lifeline of hope.

Desma's father, Brett Pugh, was the first to volunteer with MADD Avalon after Matthew's death, and Desma was grateful that he was getting involved. She began to wonder how the local chapter of MADD could ever help her and if she could help them. Her question was answered on the day of the sentencing of the driver who killed Matthew.

Desma walked into the packed courtroom and saw the offender facing the judge. She also saw the red MADD T-shirts and the concerned, solemn volunteers listening to the proceedings. The MADD Avalon chapter members had decided to come and show their support. Suddenly, she didn't feel so alone and said a silent thank you to those members. It was then that she knew just how much she and Rod needed support.

Two years after Matthew's death, Rod and Desma were asked if they would like to attend a national candlelight vigil and victims' weekend. They had many questions, and after meeting with two local MADD members, Christine Care and Sharon Clarke, Desma realized that this was something that might help her. On April 26, 2007, they attended their first national candlelight vigil in Vancouver, BC.

Desma was nervous as they stood in the hotel lobby waiting to register, but sensed only calmness around her. MADD Canada's Ardene Vicioso was there to greet them with a big smile on her face and immediately put them at ease. Soon they were meeting other victim families and more wonderful, supportive people who wanted to help. Desma began calling them her MADD family. One couple they met was from Labrador. Bella and Clarence Burden had lost their fifteen-year-old son, Damien, in an alcohol-related crash. The boys were born the same year and died the same year. Bella said that they would be forever connected by their hearts, and Desma realized how true this was. The couples spent a lot of time together that weekend and developed a close friendship.

The sessions that Rod and Desma attended during the vigil were emotionally exhausting but helpful to them. There was a session on the loss of a child and another on the legal system, given by our director of legal policy, Professor Robert Solomon. They came away with information but more importantly with hope and a newfound sense that they were not alone—that others shared their pain and were there for them. They had become a part of the MADD family.

In September 2009, Desma attended her first national MADD Canada leadership conference with Christine Care. The leadership conferences are not specifically about the victims but are training sessions for volunteers. It is here that volunteers learn how to make their local chapters as successful as possible. I had a chance to speak with Desma again at that conference, and noticed a change in her from our meeting in the fall of 2008. She was so different. Of course I still saw her sadness, which will probably be there forever, but it was tempered with a quiet strength and a determination to be of help to others. Desma had found a place, a home in our organization. We talked for a bit, laughed, cried just a little, and with a parting hug, promised to get together again.

While at that conference, Desma learned about random breath testing (RBT) during a presentation by Professor Solomon at which the Canadian Justice Minister, Hon. Rob Nicholson, was also in attendance. Random breath testing is widely accepted to be one of the most effective means of decreasing impaired driving and dramatically reducing impairment-related deaths and injuries. The introduction of RBT would be a major step forward for Canada in reducing alcohol-related crashes, giving police a valuable tool in apprehending impaired drivers who currently escape detection.

What it would mean for drivers is that they would be asked for a breath sample at occasional roadside checks. If they had unacceptable levels of alcohol in their breath sample they would be taken for further testing. It would mean that the likelihood of getting caught driving impaired would increase, and that numbers of impaired drivers would go down, resulting in fewer injuries and deaths.

Right now, these numbers are just not going down. People are not getting the message, or just have an "it won't happen to me" attitude. Yet, more people are dying or being injured by impaired drivers every day.

Professor Solomon told us that in a 2006 survey, criminal charge and conviction data indicated that a person would have to drive impaired, on average, once a week for more than three years before being charged with an impaired driving offence, and for over six years before ever being convicted. This information shocked our members and Desma as well.

We were disturbed to hear that Canada has one of the poorest impaired driving records among comparable developed democracies, even though most of those countries have higher rates of per capita alcohol consumption. RBT has been introduced in the great majority of comparable, developed democracies and has resulted in significant reductions in impaired driving crashes, fatalities, and injuries. These countries had safer roads!

For example, in Queensland, Australia, RBT is estimated to have reduced total fatal crashes by thirty-five percent, and the New South Wales RBT program is estimated to have prevented 522 serious crashes, 204 fatal crashes, and 686 single-vehicle nighttime crashes in its first year. In Ireland, the introduction of RBT in 2006 was found to have reduced total annual road fatalities by nineteen percent.

The entire audience was shocked, and some, like Desma and I, took this information very personally. If RBT had been implemented in Canada twenty years ago, as it was in Australia, could our children's lives have been among those saved? How much different would our own lives be? We encouraged our members to act on this information and contact their MPs to make sure that RBT became law in Canada. Unfortunately, as of January 2011 there have been no developments in this fight.

After hearing about RBT, Desma couldn't wait to prepare her letter and send it to all the local, provincial, and federal politicians in

Newfoundland. She even sent one to the prime minister. The conference made her realize that she does have a voice, and she became Matthew's voice.

Desma was given the opportunity to do even more to honour Matthew's memory, and at Christmas she recorded a MADD public service announcement for her local radio station. While she sat in the chair to tape the message she silently fought the urge to scream. She was so passionate and she wanted the people who heard her message to realize that Matthew was her whole world. He was too young to die and had so much to offer. His precious life was gone in seconds because of someone else's actions.

Desma taped the commercial, hoping that her message was heard.

The following April, in 2010, Desma attended her second national candlelight vigil and looked forward to seeing her whole MADD family once again. She says it was much easier the second time. Everyone provided her with comfort and words of encouragement and I'm sure that she had words of hope for all the new victims. They shared "tons of tears and miles of smiles" and when she left the vigil, once again, she came home a little stronger.

That's why MADD Canada hosts these weekends. We can't change the past, but maybe we can make a difference in how victims heal, give them a little hope for the future and a place where they can do something and not just sit, quietly accepting what has been done to them.

As for Desma's Facebook updates, it's nice to see them changing. She writes about shopping trips with nieces and family, and travelling with her husband, and shares photos of her beautiful province. And, of course, she occasionally posts just *Missing Matthew*.

* * *

MADD Canada Victim Services volunteers (VSVs) approach victims in several ways. We are always very considerate of the family and their feelings. If we hear about a crash involving alcohol or drugs and know someone in the family, it's easy to leave a card giving some contact information. We leave cards at funeral homes and sometimes police will give a card if they think it's appropriate.

Then it's left to the victim or their family to contact MADD. They talk to Gloria or the local VSV and get the information booklets that we have available. The local VSV will work with the victim and under Gloria's supervision help determine what the new victim needs in the way of support. More and more chapters have small bereavement groups that meet and share their experiences and feelings. It's important to note that we are not professional grief counsellors but volunteers. If we see that someone needs the help of a professional we will direct them toward that help.

The Annual Candlelight Vigil of Hope and Remembrance and Victims' Weekend is often the starting point of a victim's healing, and is the most valuable tool MADD Canada has to help victims.

Each and every victim is different, and their needs are just as varied. In the end every victim has to move one day at a time toward a day when the pain becomes tolerable and life becomes worth living again.

CHAPTER 7

A Tale of Two Brothers

At one of our last national victim weekends, I had the opportunity to meet a couple who arrived near the end of the victim tributes, upset because they had missed the reading of their son's tribute due to heavy local traffic. MADD Canada displayed the photo and said the words of tribute again so they could honour their baby boy, Alex, who had been killed by a suspected impaired driver. I was introduced to Mary Rodrigues-Fleming and her husband, Mike Fleming, and told them how glad we were that they could make it and wished them Godspeed as they left the conference centre to return to their family waiting at home.

When Mary heard that I was writing a book with victim stories she was one of the first to contact me. I think I forgot to breathe as I read her story through my tears; it was a tough night. But of course it was nothing compared to what she had been through.

Mary and Mike are a busy couple from Woodstock, Ontario. They have two little boys, Max and Ethan, born thirteen months apart. On May 19, 2008 (Victoria Day), Max and Ethan got to say hello to their little brother, Alexander, for the first time.

Max had just recently turned four years old and Ethan was about to turn three. Mary was a little unsure as to how they would accept Alexander. The boys were so close to each other and so close to their parents; would they be willing to share their love with a new baby? As it turns out, they were more than willing to take him under their wings.

They were so proud to have him as their younger brother that they would show him off to anyone. They fiercely defended him and his name. To them he was "Baby Alex," not just Alex or Alexander, and they would emphatically correct anyone who said it wrong. They loved to help their parents take care of Baby Alex, whether during diaper changes or while getting him ready to go out. When Alex was old enough to start eating pablum, Max and Ethan were there, ready to help.

In September, Max started junior kindergarten and was gone all day. That gave Ethan the opportunity to be the sole big brother, a role he thoroughly enjoyed. He would do just about anything to entertain Alex and would be there in a heartbeat to try and comfort him if he cried. He would pat him on the head and say, "There, there, Baby Alex. It's okay."

Thanksgiving weekend that year was beautiful, with perfect weather. On Saturday the family attended a small reunion where the boys got to play with some of their cousins, aunts, and uncles. Sunday was a quiet day at their home because Mike had to work. Mary and the boys spent the day together collecting different types and colours of leaves to celebrate autumn. While collecting the leaves they also took the opportunity to go around and greet their neighbours. Everyone commented on how big Alex was getting. Just shy of turning five months, Alex was already trying to sit up and crawl and could turn over on his own. He was showing signs of being an early achiever, much like his brothers, and he was also very vocal.

For the previous two weeks Mary had slowly been doing renovations to the kitchen and was close to being finished. So on Monday, instead of having to cook something simple for Thanksgiving dinner, she thought it would be nice if they all went out instead.

She nursed, fed, and changed Alex before they left. They had a nice dinner and Mary rocked Alex to sleep at the restaurant shortly before leaving to go home.

A few blocks from home, they stopped at a red light. When it turned green Mary began to drive through the intersection. All of a sudden Mike yelled a warning to watch out. Mary turned to her left and saw headlights, then heard metal crunching. She was in and out of consciousness for the next few minutes. She had no idea that Mike had taken the boys out of the car. Mary couldn't move. She was pinned in the car and the next thing she knew an off-duty firefighter was in the back seat of the car, behind her, talking to her and keeping her head still. He told her that everyone else was fine and that Alex had been taken to the hospital just as a precaution.

Mary knew that her injuries were not serious because she could move her feet, but the paramedics and firefighters didn't want to take any chances, so after they freed her from the car, they strapped her to a board.

When she got to the hospital, Mary immediately saw Mike and asked how Alex was. He said something along the lines of, "He will get better." Her heart sank because of the way he said it and she knew that something was seriously wrong.

Eventually both Alex and Mary were transferred from Woodstock General Hospital to London Health Sciences Centre. Alex went first, and when Mary asked to see him before he left, there were so many machines hooked up to him that she couldn't even see a hand or a foot. Mary was transferred less than an hour later, but it was still another one to two hours after she got to London before she was allowed to see him. His small body was hooked up to many machines, and tubes and IVs were attached to every limb. Mary wasn't allowed to hold him, and when she kissed her baby's head and held his hand he felt cold.

Only a few hours later, Alex's eyes stopped responding to light. Doctors quickly did a CAT scan and the neurologist told them that Alex's brain stem had been severed. The priest baptized him and gave him his last rites. At six in the morning, eleven hours after the crash, Baby Alex was pronounced dead. Five days shy of five months. He was born on a holiday and died on a holiday.

Now Mary and Mike had to go home and try to explain to Max and Ethan that their little brother was never coming home. The long ride back to Woodstock gave Mary enough time to read the literature that the social worker from the hospital had given them, explaining how to talk to children about death and grief. When they saw the boys they took them upstairs, away from the family and friends that were quickly filling up their home. The boys had sensed that something terrible had happened but they were not ready to accept it. So rather than trying to force them to talk about it, Mike and Mary brought them back downstairs. Later on that night after everyone had left they were able to tell their sons about Alex's death. Ethan buried himself in Mike's arms as if he was holding on for dear life. Max just kept saying, "Don't cry, Mommy. You don't cry, okay Mommy? You don't cry."

A couple of weeks later a friend of Mary's dropped off a book called *Henry and Harriet.* It is a beautiful story about two caterpillars who become sweethearts until one day Harriet is no longer there. The book follows Henry's emotions as he comes to accept that Harriet must have become a butterfly and will never come back. It also details Harriet's emotions as she misses Henry but goes off to explore a whole new world that she never knew existed.

As Mary read the book to Max, she explained that they were feeling like Henry and that Alex was like Harriet. At the end of the book Max turned to Mary and said that he wanted to be a butterfly like Alex. It took every bit of strength that Mary had not to break down and cry. Instead she told him that he wouldn't become a butterfly for a very long time and hugged him close.

Mary had been in contact with Gloria Appleby many times, but after reading the book with Max, she called Gloria, this time to recommend *Henry and Harriet*. Gloria quickly looked it up online and ordered it, and then she recommended that the local chapters purchase one for their lending libraries. At least thirty chapters purchased a copy. The kind act that someone did for the family has now helped many other families talk to their children about death and validate their feelings of loss.

Children see things a way an adult never could. They have a simplicity and a directness that we seem to outgrow. When Max and Ethan first saw Alex's closed casket, they called it a treasure chest. After all, it was the right size and shape. Every time they go to visit Alex at the cemetery it is to make sure that their treasure chest is still buried and safe. One day when they were visiting Alex, Max told Mary that he really missed Alex. She told him that she did too, and he said, "Then let's go get him." How Mary wished that she could agree, but instead she had to remind him that Alex was never coming home.

Mary says that she never knows when either one of the boys is going to come out with a comment or question regarding Alex or the crash. The comments are always random, but Mary and Mike work hard not to avoid the questions, but rather to talk to the boys so that they will understand. Fortunately, they are old enough that they will remember Alex, but that also means that they will remember the crash. They are not old enough to understand what death is. This is something that Mike and Mary will constantly have to help them understand as they grow older.

Mary says that when other parents in the community talk to her and Mike and try to comprehend what they are going through, the most commonly asked question is "How do you do it? I don't think I could be as strong as you and Mike."

She always tells them that as a parent you instinctively put your grieving in the background because you have to be there for your other children. Mary grieves mostly in the shower and doesn't sleep well most nights, but as soon as the boys wake up in the morning it's time to be a parent again. They keep lots of pictures of all three boys around the house, along with other little reminders of Alex. But Mary says that life must go on, their children still need to grow up and have a regular routine full of love and support.

The accused driver has entered a plea of not guilty, so the family has a long way to go before that aspect of Alex's death is resolved. Fortunately, they have a huge support system between family, friends, their community, and MADD Canada.

One of the things the community has done to show their continued support is to place stuffed animals on the light post close to where the family's car stopped. Just before Easter the year after the crash, the animals were removed by the city. A few weeks later more stuffed animals with messages appeared on the light post, and on what would have been Alex's first birthday it was inundated with animals. They have not been removed.

Every day Mary goes through that intersection, as it's right by Ethan and Max's school. To her, a little piece of Alex was left there, so every time she goes through it and sees all the animals it is like she gets to be with him again, if only for a brief moment.

From that roadside memorial came the idea of the Baby Alex Teddy Bear Drive, an annual event in which hundreds of bears are collected in several locations and are donated to a local children's hospital. Focusing on the teddy bear drive helps the family feel like they are doing something—that they are acting, not reacting. They also get to talk about their baby and how he died. His life is still affecting others. Baby Alex will not be forgotten.

Mary says that she is constantly meeting new people in her community, and when they realize who she is, the mother of the baby boy who was killed by a suspected impaired driver, they tell Mary how Alex's death affected them. People often become overwhelmed as they share their feelings and Mary feels that she has to apologize for upsetting them and tries to make them feel better. She continues to be very humbled and moved by how many lives Alex has touched. He was just a baby, but he was a baby whose life and death changed many lives.

Mary continues to speak to Gloria when she needs some support, and she has started to volunteer with the local London, Ontario, chapter. Last year and again this year she has spoken at the Project Red Ribbon launch at a high school in her area. She tells the students about her children, about Baby Alex, and about the night he was killed. She shares the pain that she lives with each day and knows that she has reached the students when she hears the sniffles in the quiet auditorium.

Mary's journey has been similar to many others. She made that first call to MADD Canada and received some much-needed support. She has been able to go to a national candlelight vigil, and she has gotten involved at a local level with MADD Canada.

She feels that by telling the story of her little boy to whoever will listen, she can make a difference in her community. Mary is right, and there is no doubt that she is making a difference. Anyone who hears her story will remember Baby Alex.

Her sons and husband give her what she needs every day—hugs and kisses and the warmth and support that love brings. The boys in their innocence and inquisitiveness can initiate some very emotional conversations, but they are her hope and inspiration for the future.

Mary's passion is the teddy bear drive, but she has also honoured Alex in another way. She is writing books for young people about a baby who dies and becomes an angel who helps others. She has given Alexander life through her stories. They sound so exciting and I can't wait for them to become public.

Mary is positive in her outlook. She knows that every day will bring new challenges and new experiences, which will join her memories of Alex in her heart.

As I reflect on Mary's journey, I realize that even though some things are similar, many of her experiences are different as well. I had the luxury of being able to immerse myself in my own grief and work quickly towards my relationship with MADD Canada. Mary hasn't had that. She had to go back to being a mother of young children first. I can't imagine her trip back from the hospital, trying to find the best way to tell her other two children that their baby brother had died. She's never had the opportunity to be just a grieving parent. Still, she's done what she can to help others as well. She shared the book that helped her children, she's shared her experiences with others, and she keeps her son's memory alive in ways that make her happy. This has been her path to healing.

It has been said that life is a journey and not a destination. The same can be said of grief. No one goes from start to finish in a straight line; grief is like a maze.

We follow the path we think is right. Sometimes it works out, but often our path is blocked by unforeseen obstacles and we have to backtrack, rethink, and again move forward. Sometimes someone will help us through, and other times we go it alone. The important thing is that we don't give up. Eventually, in time, we each find our own way.

The unique thing about MADD Canada victim services is that the organization does recognize individuality in the healing process. MADD victim services are provided by volunteers who often have themselves been victims. Sometimes they can share their own experiences, or, if it is more appropriate, just be there to listen and understand. As Mary told me, sometimes friends try to help but can't deal with all the anger and pain. MADD has been there, and its volunteers can help.

Meeting people like Mike and Mary meant so much to me in my role as national president. All victims need someone to relate to, so I tell Bruce's story when I can to give a sense of shared experiences. It's what makes victims feel at home and for that I am grateful. It's the best part of what I do.

For anyone who has been a victim of impaired driving, all it takes to get help is one call to MADD Canada. It doesn't matter if the crash was yesterday or thirty years ago. If you or someone you love is a victim, MADD Canada wants you to call. They can help. (Information on how to reach MADD Canada can be found on page 184 of this book.)

Just calling the help line is so easy; chances are, if you call, you will speak with Gloria. Maybe that's as far as you will decide to go. Gloria will also look for someone in your local area to speak with you and direct you to a local chapter if that is what you want.

Maybe you want to take part in the online memorial or the national memorial wall, or maybe you just want someone to listen. MADD follows your lead.

Getting involved or being a member may not be what you want, and that is perfectly fine. A call to MADD is not you making any kind of commitment. It's about MADD Canada making a commitment to you, to help with your healing in any way possible.

For me, getting involved was the basis for my healing. Fighting back in whatever way I could. If that meant giving out ribbons or setting up a mall display or sending an email to my MP, I did it. There is no limit to what you can do, but there are also no expectations or obligations.

CHAPTER 8

The Seventh Sister

In April 2009, I met the Linehan sisters. It was my second national victims' weekend as national president. Every year it's hard to see the raw grief on the faces of new delegates, because we know they have a long road ahead. Then my emotions do a flip because it's such a pleasure to see the returning delegates come in with a smile on their faces and hugs for their MADD family.

On these occasions I can't help but think back to my first national victims' weekend and how I felt coming through those doors for the first time. Now I want to be there for new victims, and that April I was determined to meet as many as possible. They had become part of our family, the family of impaired driving victims—a family that no one wants to join.

I saw Gloria as she welcomed delegates who were just arriving. Many were returning delegates who had become old friends. Many new faces would be friends by the time the weekend was over.

The non-discriminatory nature of impaired driving became apparent with each new delegate that arrived, whether from the east coast, the west coast, or from the north; from Toronto, Vancouver, or Conception Bay, Newfoundland. And so many had that look.

It was the look I see in my pictures from the first year after I lost Bruce. The light in their eyes was gone, and only the question remained: "Why?" They hoped that MADD Canada could provide the answer.

Soon, I heard a familiar accent and noticed three beautiful young women who had joined the conference. Their Newfoundland accent brought an automatic smile to my face. If you've ever known a Newfoundlander, you know what I mean; they are, with few exceptions, the happiest, funniest, and most easygoing people in our country. They have a love of life that is contagious. When these women smiled, however, their smiles were mixed with tears. I later learned their names were Doris, Florence, and Edith Linehan. They had lost their brother Roger just a few short months before, on Boxing Day of 2008. They laughed and cried as they called him their seventh sister. They told a story of love, family, and loss that touched us all.

The Linehans were raised in a small community called Admirals Beach in St. Mary's Bay, Newfoundland. With pride Edith told me that Admirals Beach was resettled from Great Colinet Island, which in turn had been settled by their Irish ancestors during the potato famine.

Their brother Roger was the eighth of nine children and loved everything about his rich Irish Newfoundland heritage—the music, the songs, the stories, and the dances. It was from that culture that he inherited his wonderful ability to tell a well-embellished story. Edith said that Roger had a natural talent for making anyone laugh, and he was always the life of the party.

The eldest two of the Linehan family were boys, and then came the girls. Five sisters were older than Roger, and the last one, Doris, was younger. Roger grew up with the girls and loved it. He listened to their whispered boyfriend stories and his sisters' dilemmas about fashion and hairstyles.

Women loved him. He was six feet tall with a body made for hugs. His smile lit up the room, but you could see the mischief in his eyes. He always knew what to say, how to say it, and when to say it. Still, the sisters laughed, for he always seemed to be in one kind of a scrape or other with his female friends.

When he needed some sisterly help he would talk to Doris or Edith. The trouble is, he would do such a great job of telling the story, exaggerated or not, that they'd be laughing too hard—to the point of tears, often—to help him.

One such story was about a time when he planned to entertain a lady at his apartment. He wanted to impress this woman, so he went all out. He asked Doris to recommend expensive wine so he could share a drink with his date after dinner. He created a romantic ambiance and prepared the meal with great care. Confident in his attention to detail, he felt ready for a magnificent evening with his lovely lady.

Roger described the scene to his sisters. He told them he had the mood set with the lights dimmed and scented candles lit. He arranged things on the coffee table to make himself look really intelligent— political books and *National Geographic*.

His lady friend arrived and he seated her by the table to enjoy a lovely meal. Everything was going smoothly; the conversation was interesting, the meal was delicious, and the atmosphere was cozy. Then Roger realized he had forgotten music. Yes, he thought, soft music in the background with that expensive red wine would be just the touch. As he got up from his chair to put on the music, his lady friend was sipping her wine and smiling at him. He was so pleased! This was going to be a wonderful night.

At that moment, he accidentally hit her elbow, making her spill red wine all over her designer white pants. He tried to comfort and reassure her that the stain could be removed and in doing so he gently stroked her hair with his hand. His watchstrap became entangled in her hair. "Just my luck," Roger described to his sisters. His date became visibly annoyed with him. "I nearly hauled the head off 'er."

After freeing her hair from his watch and cleaning the mess from the wine, the mood was gone. He spent the remainder of the night at the dry cleaners'. He said, in a well-embellished accent, "The only thing I got out of that was an empty wallet."

When Roger was retelling this incident he had his sisters in gales of laughter. He would use exaggerated gestures to animate the scene and asked Edith to fill in as his date as he demonstrated. There were times during her acting when Edith could hardly stand up because she was laughing so much.

They all had so much fun and their lives were so full of promise for the future. They had no reason to think it would ever end.

Roger was a great brother and had a gentle and thoughtful side that he reserved for his family and close friends. Edith told us about Christmas in their home and her descriptions of her brother and the way he had with his sisters brought tears to my eyes. Their love for him is so obvious. They miss him so much.

Christmas was always the high point of the year for the Linehan family. Every year the sisters would get together for a night with just the sisters and no families. They called it their annual PJ party. Roger was always the first to arrive. He made sure they didn't have it without him, and he stayed in the same room so he didn't miss a thing. He'd say that they were having a sleepover and proudly referred to himself as "The Seventh Sister." That little bit of childhood followed them throughout their lives, through marriage and children, good times and bad. How glad they are now to have these precious memories to share.

Roger was in all ways their "Seventh Sister," and their hearts ache at the void left in their lives.

Christmas of 2008 was supposed to be great. Edith and her two sons were headed to Nova Scotia to spend the holiday with her sister Doris. From St. John's to Halifax is not such a long flight, but it was diverted to Toronto because of a horrendous snowstorm. Once they were in Toronto they were told that there were no available flights to Halifax until December 26. This was not what they had hoped for and it seemed their holiday would be spent away from family in a hotel room. Luckily, the airlines found them seats the next day and they made it to Halifax and Doris's waiting and anxious arms in time for Christmas.

Their holiday had started badly, but they all felt the worst was behind them and now they could relax. On Boxing Day they decided to go to a movie. As they pulled into the garage, Doris's cell phone rang. It was a strange number, but Doris recognized the area code as being from Newfoundland, so she answered. There was a screaming from the other end of the line and the words didn't make sense. She passed the phone to Edith, who recognized Roger's girlfriend's voice saying, "Roger is dead!"

Edith thought that there must have been some mistake. She had just talked to Roger the day before. But Roger's girlfriend answered her questions and told her that the police had just left after telling her that Roger had been hit by a car.

Edith felt like someone had punched her in the stomach and she couldn't breathe. She still wanted to believe there had been some kind of mistake, that someone must have the wrong information— that it was the other person who was dead, not Roger. Anyone, just not Roger.

The sisters finally accepted that yes, indeed it was their brother who had died, and their only thoughts were about getting home. But first, Edith had the horrible job of letting everyone know what had happened. Many of her siblings were away for the holidays, but one by one she reached them and passed on the terrible news.

Of course, it was almost impossible trying to get home during the Christmas season. There were no immediate flights available and the sisters spent an endlessly long night together. Sleep evaded them and they spent their time together crying, remembering, sometimes laughing, and then crying again.

It seemed impossible to think that Roger wouldn't be at the airport to meet them with that grin on his face pretending that he just happened to be at the airport that day; often if they'd been on vacation or if Doris was coming home to visit, Roger would be waiting at the arrivals gate and pretend he'd just been driving by the airport and decided to drop in.

The sisters couldn't understand how he could have been in a crash. Roger was a cautious driver; they used to tease him that he drove too slowly and carefully, like their father. They knew that road conditions were good that night and they knew that Roger would never drink and drive. They were mystified. What could have happened to their brother?

Soon they found out that Roger's vehicle had been struck by a drunk driver travelling on the wrong side of the median. Roger didn't have a chance. He was hit head-on and was killed almost instantly. He was taken to the hospital by ambulance but there was nothing that could be done to revive him. Their funny, harmless, gentle brother was gone forever and their family would never feel whole again.

They discovered that the man responsible for the crash, the drunk driver, also killed himself that night. Edith said that when she found out she began to shake all over with repulsion and rage. She felt glad that the driver had died. She didn't feel remorse, guilt, or sadness for him, and she still doesn't. It shocks her. Before Roger's death she would never have voiced such thoughts. Her Catholic conscience would have bothered her too much. Roger's death has changed Edith and she finds it difficult to understand how one person could drive drunk and have so little regard for human life. To her it is beyond comprehension.

The sisters came home to Newfoundland, and the brothers and sisters were reunited. Never had the love of family been so needed, though now the missing piece became even more obvious.

Going to the funeral home made it all so real. It was obscene to see Roger lying in that casket, to see their healthy, vibrant brother lying so lifeless. It was Christmas, a time for family. It shouldn't have been a time of death. The Linehans were awed by the sheer number of friends and family who came to honour Roger and show their support with comfort, tears, and hugs.

Among the mourners was Desma Churchill, who, having lost her son, Matthew, to a drunk driver, understood their pain. She came to offer her support to their family, even though they were strangers to her, and offered selfless understanding. Florence suggested that maybe they should reach out to MADD for help and support, but Edith was so upset and angry at the time that she couldn't see any sense in her sister's suggestion. She couldn't imagine that MADD could help them with anything.

A few months later, Christine Care, the MADD Avalon chapter president, approached them about going to the national victims' weekend in Ontario. The family recognized that they did need help and started to seek out more information about MADD. The mission statement—to stop impaired driving and support victims of this violent crime—spoke to the sisters. Doris, Florence, and Edith decided to accept Christine's invitation, even though they were unsure if they could handle it emotionally.

It was a weekend they would not forget. The sisters went to every seminar they could possibly fit into the two days. The second night was the Candlelight Vigil of Hope and Remembrance. Their brother, Dermot, and his wife came from Whitby to join them for the service. Edith remembers that night and the beauty of the service as candles were lit for each victim that had been killed or injured. She also remembers having a terrible headache from crying so much during the day.

When Roger's smiling face filled the screen and they stood as a family to honour their brother and listen to the words they had chosen as their personal tribute to him, Edith's legs were weak. It was one of the hardest things she had ever done, but in the end, Edith was proud that she was there to remember him.

The conference was both draining and rewarding. Doris, Florence, and Edith remember all the incredible people they met and those who shared their heart-wrenching stories. Not once did the sisters feel uncomfortable about crying whenever grief overwhelmed them, and they felt free to express their feelings about Roger without fear of making someone else uncomfortable. It was a great release.

The weekend wasn't all sadness. At night before they retired to bed they would gather in one room to reminisce about Roger. All too soon, they would be roaring with laughter. That episode would be followed with tears, and soon they would think of another one of his scrapes and gales of laughter would erupt again. For them it was wonderful therapy.

The sisters say that at the conference there was always someone around to give a word of encouragement or just to listen to them. Edith says that the wonderful people at MADD knew what they wanted and needed even before they did. She found the entire event very well organized. It exceeded all of their expectations, and she was totally amazed at the devotion and dedication of the volunteers and organizers during their stay. It was a crucial step to helping them on their journey…a journey that they realize will never end. It just changes.

How pleased I was to hear that we at MADD Canada had succeeded in our desire to help these victims on their way, not to recovery, but to seeing that life would still go on and they would someday feel better.

I asked Edith what she has learned from her experience, the death of her brother and her experience with MADD Canada's victim support.

She said that Roger's death was so unexpected and sudden that she just wasn't prepared for it. He had so much to live for, and she took it for granted that he would always be there. This tragedy was life altering for her. Her own difficulty in dealing with Roger's death and the way it has affected those around her has been overwhelming. She remembers being unable to drive for weeks after Roger's death. She was terrified of other drivers and once she actually got behind the wheel she felt her heart racing and was constantly hesitating whenever she was in a turning lane. Edith felt that the headlights of each oncoming car were pointed at her and was sure that she would be in a collision. Fear is a terrible thing to live with, and when we are traumatized so deeply, our minds and bodies react without reason.

Edith had always felt that their family would be together for a long time, never giving death a second thought. However, that has changed; now she wonders who will be next. She is overly cautious with her children. She questions whether she should let her youngest son walk home at night like he used to or whether she should allow her oldest to ride in the car with his friends. The second-guessing never stops. She doesn't like what this has done to her.

I sympathize with her fear. Mine was especially bad immediately after Bruce's death, but even now, sometimes I still have an irrational fear of things that otherwise would have been routine—saying goodbye at my back door; seeing my daughter go down the driveway or my husband leave for work. What if something happens again? Would I survive it a second time? Then I shake my head and put it out of my mind. It can't happen again. Can it?

Edith believes that she is too emotional still to volunteer with MADD; after all, healing doesn't happen in one weekend. At the conference she and her sisters were given the tools, the information on how to deal with their loss, and the advice from others who have been in the same place. They now know that they are not alone, and if they find they need any additional help they can contact Christine Care, or the local Victim Service Volunteer, or Gloria at the national office.

MADD Canada Victim Services is glad to have been there for the Linehan sisters, and I hope I will see them again sometime soon. I'd love to hear more of Roger's blarney, and maybe I'll get to share some of Bruce's antics too.

CHAPTER 9

Sharing the Journey

There are people who have shared my journey, and I've not always been aware of them by my side. Some were there at Bruce's funeral or knew Bruce before he was killed. Some have watched with interest as I became involved with MADD Canada but not introduced themselves to me until our lives intersected and our interests put us on the same path.

Sharon Mitchell is one such person. When I first met Sharon, she was a former Halifax police officer and was working as a policing consultant for the Justice Department. The first time we talked was in 2006 at Operation Christmas, a Nova Scotia initiative that includes officers from many levels of law enforcement. Sharon had seen our family at Bruce's funeral and had known Bruce as a police officer while he was in Springhill. She was part of that solemn group of officers that helped us lay our son to rest on May 20, 2004.

Sharon is a woman in a predominantly male world, and the fact that she is blond and beautiful with a big smile and striking personality probably makes it even harder to gain the respect of her peers. She could easily be dismissed as a stereotype, but anyone who casually dismisses Sharon will soon learn a lesson.

She proved herself a very capable police officer, and with a lot of hard work rose through the ranks in her professional career until she was offered an amazing opportunity with the Nova Scotia Department of Justice. Sharon had an unusual story to tell me, and I had heard that she had even once been hit by a drunk driver, back when she was entering her career in law enforcement. Luckily she had no lingering effects from that crash and that driver was prosecuted for impaired driving.

After I was named MADD Canada's national president in 2007, we met again, this time in Nova Scotia's transportation minister's office. Also at the meeting were Premier Rodney MacDonald; the transportation minister, Angus MacIssac; and the justice minister and attorney general, our friend Murray Scott. They asked Susan MacAskill and I to come so they could present "Vision 2012," the Nova Scotia government's goal towards reducing the number of lives lost on our provincial highways. It was a good presentation, and the fact that they were asking us to endorse their program made me realize that the province has a lot of respect for MADD Canada.

Afterward Sharon came and told me how pleased she was that I had been named the president of MADD Canada. We shared a teary minute as she reminded me how proud Bruce would have been. I knew I had a strong ally and looked forward to hearing from her again. About once or twice a year our paths would cross, and when in the spring of 2008 I heard that she and her son were recovering from a serious impaired driving crash, I wrote to her immediately.

"Tell me it's not so," I wrote. "I've heard a rumour but pray that it's wrong. What happened?" Soon I heard back from her, and her words chilled me to the bone.

Sharon told me that she had been involved in a crash on March 15, 2008.

It was a slushy kind of day. Ryan and Sharon were driving to his hockey game at the Bowles Arena in Dartmouth. They had a lot to discuss on the way there. After all, not only was it his sister, Samantha's, sixteenth birthday, but it was St. Patrick's Day as well, an Irish tradition celebrated by their family. The conversation turned to strategy as they got closer to the rink—they needed to discuss defensive plays and how they were going to beat this team for a gold medal.

They stopped at the red light beside the old Moirs chocolate factory. With a smile, Ryan turned to his mom and mentioned that he wished they could still get chocolate there. Sharon laughed and reminded him that his sweet tooth would get the best of him someday. As the light turn green, Sharon proceeded slowly through the intersection.

It was then she saw a car coming…racing…accelerating. It seemed like everything around them slowed down, and Sharon felt like she had a week's worth of thoughts in what must have been seconds. Foremost was the realization that the driver was not going to stop and was trying to turn in front of them. "Shit!" is the last thing she recalls saying out loud.

Her police training and mother's protective instincts took over as she threw her arm across her son's chest and turned her vehicle so at the very least the oncoming vehicle would hit her side. The sound of metal on metal filled the air.

Sharon remembers how quiet everything was after the crash. She is still not sure if it was a dream or real, but everything was white. It was like sitting in the middle of a snow-covered field with no one around for miles. She thought then that she had better not be dead, and that she would be cranky if she were.

All of that changed quickly. The quiet serenity turned into sounds of terror. Screams, the kind that every mother knows—the screams of a terrified and hurt child.

"Mom! Mom! Please, Mom, wake up. Please don't die." Sharon could feel Ryan's hands on her shoulder and every nurturing, protective, motherly instinct amplified. The pain in her face and chest seemed surreal. Sharon felt like she could move mountains for her son at that point, but the reality was that she could barely breathe. She reached for Ryan and tried to speak but nothing came out. At the same time she could hear people outside her car calling to them, asking if they were all right. She struggled to take a deep breath, but then turned to her son and finally spoke. "It's okay, buddy. I am here. I got you. Take my hand." Over and over she kept trying to reassure him.

Most of Sharon's memory of this time is fragmented. Her flashes of recollection were filled in later with details from others. Like a movie, screen by screen, clip by clip, she has flashes and images that have returned slowly over time: The familiar face of an RCMP officer she had worked with a few times who happened to be off-duty and at the intersection. The truck driver who was on his cellphone, calling for help. The look of panic on her son's face. The tears streaming down his cheeks and the eyes begging her for the help she wasn't able to give.

She couldn't hold him. She couldn't comfort him. She was pinned in the car and could not move.

She was also thinking about her daughter, who was celebrating her birthday with a girls' sleepover. Sharon didn't want this to be the day Samantha got bad news. Ever the mom, her heart pained with the thought.

Sharon struggles with one memory of the crash, and that memory brings back all the hostility and fury of that day. It was of watching the other driver—a human being who had no regard for the life of her son, herself, or anyone on the road that day—get out of his car and walk towards them. Sharon has been told she was cursing at him, telling him to get the f— away from the car. Then she turned to the RCMP officer and told him that the driver was drunk. She was sure of it.

She still has little memory of the rest of the crash scene—the fire-fighters, paramedics, police. She does not recall her son trying to pry his door open and trying to get them out of the vehicle. There was smoke coming from the engine and Ryan was terrified the car was going to catch fire.

Sharon has been spared any recollection of her initial pain as paramedics got her out of the car and secured her on a back board, of having her son by her side in the ambulance as the paramedics worked on her, or her repeated message to Ryan that she was okay and that what was happening was routine. In fact, she repeated the message forty or fifty times, and it's become a family joke, one of those light moments that can came from the darkest times.

Her next memory is of her boyfriend, Dan, as he looked down into her eyes with concern. Dan is a Halifax police officer and was on duty when the call came in. He rushed to be at Sharon's side. A fellow hockey mom, Kathy, came to the hospital. Sharon was on the stretcher in the hall and feeling panicky since she did not know where her son was. She felt like she was calling out, asking for Ryan, and yet she wondered where she was, why no one could hear or see her. It was then that Kathy leaned over and told Sharon that she was there and would stay with Ryan until his father got there. Finally, Sharon could let go and burst into tears. She knew that no matter what happened to her, Ryan was safe and with people who cared.

Sharon didn't have an easy time in the months that followed. She recovered from head injuries that left one side of her face numb. She had severe headaches, memory loss, and back and neck injuries.

Sharon still feels angry about the accident. After countless missed days at work, endless doctors' appointments, physiotherapy, and specialists, it's still not over for her. She still suffers from memory loss, and deals with frustration every day when she can't go to the gym like she used to, can't play street hockey with the kids, can't even mow her lawn. It's frustrating to have to rely on her daughter, Sam, or her boyfriend, Dan, or other good friends to do things for her, to need their understanding when she's sore and tired, or even worse, when she's angry because this didn't need to happen. And still, nothing is worse than listening to her son wake up in the middle of the night screaming because he's having nightmares that he and his mom are burning or that he can't get out of the car.

As for the drunk driver: It's finished. It was a long process, but finally Sharon feels that justice has been served. She was in court that final day and saw the driver's remorse before he received his sentence. It helped.

And despite the occasional residual anger and frustration, Sharon feels lucky. She says that every day when she sees her amazing children, her family, and friends; when she has to pay the bills, cook dinner, clean the house, or go to work; when she has to carpool or asks her kids for the tenth time to clean their rooms...she is lucky! She tries not to allow the offender to make her more of a victim than she already is. Every day that she does not want to get up, resents going to one more medical appointment, or cries in sheer frustration, is one more day he wins—and so she goes on, living her life to the fullest and making each day count. She does it for herself, and for all those victims of impaired driving who didn't make it. She does it because if she doesn't, the impaired driver wins.

Soon after hearing about her crash, MADD Canada asked Sharon if she was interested in attending a national victims' weekend to help her deal with what had happened to her. She accepted, though like so many attendees, she didn't know what to expect. Through the weekend I often saw glimpses of her as she mingled with other delegates. I was really interested in her opinion of the conference and MADD Canada's victim support services, hoping that we would live up to her expectations. How surprised and pleased I was to get this letter a short while later:

MADD *Canada*,

I wanted to take a moment to thank you for sponsoring me and my guest to attend the MADD Canada national candlelight vigil in Toronto recently.

It was an experience that I will never forget and have difficulty writing the words that accurately describe the weekend. As someone who has spent most of her career being involved in law enforcement and more specifically road safety and issues related to impaired driving, I always had an understanding and dedication to combating impaired driving through committees, enforcement and other means. Then, as you know, my son and I had the unfortunate experience of being involved in a head-on collision with an impaired driver a year ago and it brought my understanding of this senseless act to a whole different level. That said, being involved at the candlelight vigil afforded me the opportunity to see the effects and devastation through a far greater lens. It raised my awareness to a level I never imagined.

I was overwhelmed at the amount of people [impaired driving] has affected, especially knowing that the people in attendance are simply a small group in comparison to the reality Canada and worldwide. Logically I always knew it affected a tremendous amount of individuals, but actually seeing and experiencing it up close and personal made me feel that despite my work and personal experience, I truly lived in a bubble.

I had never felt more support and compassion from a group of individuals in my life. Strangers who after a few days were life-long friends. People who would have all the right in the world to be bitter and hateful. Yet, despite their passion for addressing impaired driving and living with the effects every day through injuries or the loss of a loved one, [they] exuded strength, determination, compassion, peace, hope and the most positive outlook on life. Although some still have their struggles, and rightly so, the feeling during that weekend is one that I could not explain unless I was there, and still struggle for accurate words.

For that I thank you. I think police, public prosecution and the judiciary could learn more from that weekend than any conference or workshop could possibly offer. More so, I think every person who is charged with impaired [driving] or convicted of drinking and driving, should spend a weekend sitting through this conference. It is the personal side, the human side that educates and provides awareness. I know, because this opportunity taught me more than I had ever learned through any book, work experience or by being a living victim. I can never thank you enough.

Sincerely yours,
Sharon Mitchell

For Sharon's sake, I wish this were the end of her personal impaired driving story, but one day a few months after the conference I had another email from Sharon. It had happened again. Sharon was driving in her car with Dan through an intersection in Cole Harbour. Again, she saw a car coming toward her. She couldn't believe it was happening again and tried to back up her vehicle to avoid a collision.

This time she was successful, but several others were not. An impaired driver slammed into several cars that were stopped at the intersection. Sharon and Dan raced to the aid of one man who was buried in the rubble; Sharon held him as he took his last breath. Then she went to assist a woman whose vehicle had been thrown across the intersection. Sharon held the woman's head together with her hands as she waited for help. She later learned the victim had a broken back along with her serious head lacerations. I can only imagine Sharon's sense of *déjà vu* as emergency workers looked after the victims. Sharon shuddered as she remembered how the injured woman looked. It's truly a miracle that she lived at all. Meanwhile, the impaired driver was taken to hospital and was later charged with impaired driving causing death.

Sharon has now been there for all of it. She was a victim; she worked at this issue from a justice perspective; and now was a witness, and had the gruesome experience of having someone die in her arms and seeing the sheer carnage that this woman, the drunk driver, had caused.

None of this should have happened to her or any of the victims, but I am thankful that MADD has been there to help her as she was there for us. Sharon's strength serves as a reminder to all of us that it's so important not to give up. She will never cease in her battle to bring impaired drivers to justice. More intimate than many with the real personal cost of impaired driving, she continues to fight back and is an inspiration to all victims.

I found it surprising when I first discovered how many MADD members are police officers and first responders. It really makes you realize the impact that impaired driving has on them in their daily lives. In many cases they deal with the victims and offenders at the same time. They are the ones who go to the door and face the parents or loved ones of victims, knowing that the words they say will be etched in the minds of these people for the rest of their lives.

Victim stories have long related the impact of this first contact from police. There are many horror stories, as well as stories of compassionate and caring officers. MADD Canada, listening to these stories, found out that in most cases the officer notifying family or loved ones of the deceased had little training in death notification, and many officers felt they were unskilled in this most difficult task.

MADD Canada developed a Death Notification Training Program, and a group of retired police officers was recruited and trained by the national office. These officers provide police and victim service agencies with a better understanding of death notification and give them the tools to do a better job. This program has been used widely in Canada and ensures that death notification techniques are taught at a consistently high standard and that victims of impaired driving crashes begin their traumatic grief process with the best possible notification.

Policing is a difficult career with little thanks from the general public, but police are also the ones we turn to in need.

So, to Sharon and all those men and women in blue who protect us every day, thank you for all you do.

CHAPTER 10

The Greatest Fear

My greatest fear is of losing another child or grandchild. I'm not sure that I would survive another brush with tragedy. When I think of something happening to my daughters or my grandchildren, well...my mind won't even let me consciously go there. But sometimes the fear just won't stay locked away.

Just ask my daughter Monica. I dropped her off at the airport one day just a while ago. She was going to Costa Rica by herself to backpack for two weeks. I was a mess. It didn't matter that she is a smart, capable woman in her thirties; I was afraid. As she turned to go through customs, I asked her to turn around one last time for a photo. I wanted a recent picture so that if she went missing...well, enough said. I cried all the way to the car. I suppose I was overreacting, but the problem is that I know awful things happen. I've talked to people who have lived the experience of losing again. I've met Ben and Brenda Wright.

Ben and Brenda came to MADD Canada in 2004, but their real story started twelve years earlier.

On April 22, 1992, their son, Wayne, turned thirty. Everything in his life was coming together for him. He loved playing music and had a good job with employers who were pleased with his work. He had just bought his first house and had plans to fix it up. He was very excited about his future. This had not always been the case for him; Wayne had struggled to this point in his life and had faced many difficult hurdles along the way. But now, as he turned thirty, all this was behind him. As parents, Ben and Brenda were happy and pleased for Wayne.

On June 13, 1992, less than two months later, everything changed. Wayne had worked one and a half shifts and then visited with a friend on his way back home. When he arrived home that night he decided to work on his prized possession, his motorcycle. Wayne stayed up all night tinkering away at the bike and in the morning left his house to test-drive it. He failed to make a turn in the road, hit the shoulder, and lost control of the motorcycle. His family was told he died instantly.

Ben and Brenda were deeply traumatized. They had lost their son. They didn't know how they could go on with the rest of their lives without Wayne.

Brenda says that a whole piece of her was wrenched from her that day. She went for days, weeks, and then years in a fog, pain gripping her heart. It was frightening. She spent three years in therapy trying to find a way to cope with her awful loss.

Once in her therapy session she confided to her therapist that the child her daughter, Laura, and son-in-law, Michael, were expecting was a godsend to both her and Ben, but that Brenda was terrified of loving him too much in case she lost him. She knew that she couldn't survive another loss.

The therapist convinced Brenda that no one could predict what the future would bring and encouraged her to start trusting in life more.

Laura had been her parents' lifesaver in the years after Wayne's death. She gave much of herself to get her parents through that devastating loss even as she grieved for her brother.

Laura was a delightful child who grew into a beautiful, confident woman who never lost her ability to giggle at silly things. She was a hard worker and showed that she cared about family and friends with a simple touch, a kind word, or a smile. She cherished them. The photographs and memories that Brenda has of Laura remind her that Laura's life was bursting with hope for a marvellous future.

Laura and Brenda were always very close. Each year they went on a girls' weekend, just the two of them. Brenda remembers both of their husbands teasing, telling them not to break the bank on their shopping sprees. They would shop until they dropped, go to the theatre, and talk for hours about their hopes and dreams.

Laura's relationship with her father was just as special. She would get some project in her mind and it wouldn't take long for her to convince her father to take it on for her.

On November 7, 1993, Laura and Michael presented Ben and Brenda with their baby grandson, Jonathon. Laura remembers that time with a smile and says that Jonathon was so beautiful, and that she didn't end up being afraid to love him because love was built right into that little boy. It flowed freely from his little heart to theirs.

He became their hope for the future. Brenda says that it was impossible to describe how much joy he brought into their lives and the lives of all who knew him.

Ben and Brenda spent many hours with Michael, Laura, and Jonathon. They looked after their growing grandson as often as they could. After losing Wayne they were even more attentive and didn't want to miss one milestone in Jonathon's development.

They went to his school concerts, celebrated all the holidays with him, and took him to his soccer games. They gave him sailing lessons, hoping he would develop a love of sailing like their own. They went on outings and vacations everywhere. Once when they were leaving the museum after seeing the dinosaurs, Jonathon told them he was going to be a paleontologist. They were stunned because they didn't expect him to even know what that meant.

Jonathon wanted to be a scientist. He didn't know what kind, but he knew that was what he wanted to be. And he had the intelligence to follow through.

One of Jonathon's most uttered phrases was, "My grandpa says," and he and Ben had a very special bond. Ben loves to tell the story of an excursion that he and Jonathon took to an observatory to view the night sky. Each time the guide began to describe some planet or star, Jonathon would pipe up and name it first. Then he told the guide that he and his grampy had a special name for that one, Sagittarius. "We call it the teacup!" Jonathon loved fishing and on his last fishing trip in August 2002, he was determined to get the biggest catch. He was a star that day and his delight with his fish was a joy to see.

Jonathon also had a mischievous way about him. His laugh was infectious and he got on well with everyone. He was a leader and took the time to help others.

Laura and Jonathon got a golden retriever pup in July 2002 and named her Katie. Brenda remembers how much fun it was to watch them interact with this little dog. They loved her dearly. Katie had the run of the house and filled their lives with happiness. This was important for them, because Michael had left the family unit a few months earlier, and they were struggling to put their lives back together.

At her birthday celebration in November 2002, Laura tried to put together a drawing of a table she wanted built. They all got a good laugh at her efforts as they tried to decipher what it was she intended. Brenda had to leave early that night to curl. She didn't know that that would be the last time she would see Laura's wonderful face or hear her laugh.

Tragedy struck a few days later, on November 29, 2002. Ben and Brenda were just sitting down to dinner when the phone rang. It was Michael looking for Laura. She was supposed to meet him in Barrie with Jonathon so he could spend the weekend with his son. Laura was already two hours late. Michael said that he had called friends who might know where she was and no one had seen or heard from her.

As soon as Brenda heard that Laura was late she became very upset and had to give the phone to Ben. Ben told Michael to contact the police to see if there had been any accidents and then call him back. When Ben got off the phone Brenda began to get hysterical and kept saying over and over, "It can't have happened again, please, God, not again." The sick feeling in the pit of her stomach told her that something was wrong. Ben too felt panicked and was near tears but was trying to hold himself together.

When Michael called back he said the police had been trying to locate him, and had asked him to go to the Barrie hospital because there had been an accident.

Brenda remembers that night with such pain. All the way to Barrie she and Ben were crying and asking God to please not let this be happening. Brenda could barely control herself.

When they entered the emergency room, an officer immediately met them and asked them to go into a room off to the side. Brenda wanted to see Laura and Jonathon and tried to argue but finally relented and did as she was asked.

There Brenda saw Laura's best friend, Dennise, and her husband, Glenn. There were other people there, but she zeroed in on the couple for the answers to her questions.

"Is she gone?" Brenda asked.

"Yes, Brenda," Dennise replied. Brenda's heart shattered.

"What about the child, what about Jonathon?" she asked.

"Yes," Dennise said again.

Brenda went to Ben and they held each other without speaking. There are no words in the English language for the emotions they were experiencing. They wondered how their whole lives could disintegrate in an instant. Just like that.

Michael had gone through the death of their son, Wayne, with them so he advised the police officers and the hospital staff that Ben and Brenda would be very fragile and possibly hysterical on hearing the news of Laura and Jonathon's deaths, since this was not the first time they had lost a child.

Two police officers and a police victim services person met with Ben and Brenda. She remembers them as wonderful and kind people, there to help them in whatever way possible. Brenda was lost in her own world for a while and kept rocking back and forth, trying to comprehend what was happening. Finally she asked one of the officers how the accident had happened.

That's when they learned that the other driver had been drunk and had driven through a stop sign. Laura was killed instantly; Jonathon died a short time later.

Those two beautiful people were gone from their lives in one violent, senseless moment. The person who took their lives was seriously impaired. He knowingly got in his truck and drove when he could barely stand, and wiped out Ben and Brenda's whole family.

Ben and Brenda were more than traumatized.

How do you move on after something like this happens? That was the question that Brenda asked her husband over and over. She questioned whether it was even possible to keep on living after what had happened. Once again Brenda felt like she had lost a part of herself. She felt as if she had lost her soul.

Brenda says that there is there is no way to filling that emptiness. Pain and sadness are her constant companions; they suffocate her, pervading her every waking moment. Still today, after seven years, they grip her when she least expects it. And no wonder. She and Ben had had hopes and dreams for their children. No parent should have to bury their child.

At the funeral, many people came to share memories, to give hugs and say a kind word or two. It meant so much to the Wrights, for it gave them a glimmer of hope. Brenda feels that God truly blessed her and her husband with the ability to remember. They may have lost their children, but no one can ever take their memories.

Because the crash had been caused by an impaired driver, Ben and Brenda asked their friends to give donations to MADD Canada if they so desired.

Over the months following the crash, the police officers who had been at the scene stayed connected to them and kept them informed of the court case. Brenda can't say enough about the kindness of the police and the crown attorney throughout the court process. It was long and drawn out and ended with the person who killed Laura and Jonathon being sentenced with three years in jail, of which he served only eight months. The Wrights feel this sentence was a farce; the driver is free to live his life, but they still have to live without Laura and Jonathon.

A short time after the funeral, Michael's new wife, Tracey, contacted MADD Canada at Ben and Brenda's request; they wanted to learn how they could help stop the carnage caused by impaired driving. Their first contact was a wonderful volunteer named Joanne Gerard Simmonds from the York Region chapter. Joanne came to visit them at home and spent many hours talking with them, answering their questions, and soothing their pain. The information that Joanne left for them was very beneficial, and together they attended a few meetings of the MADD York chapter.

Shortly afterwards, they met Margaret Williams from the MADD Barrie chapter. Margaret became the couple's support throughout their court proceedings. She was there on every court date and also took the time to call Brenda to check in often. Margaret strengthened their resolve to become involved in the fight to stop impaired driving.

They started to attend meetings with the Barrie chapter, and in 2004 they went to the national victims' weekend in Toronto. They were very nervous but at the same time needed to be there to connect with others who had gone through what they had. For them it was a very moving experience. Brenda was on the verge of tears all the time, but never felt alone.

It was during that weekend that Brenda began to believe that she might be able to contribute to MADD Canada through victim services. She was not emotionally ready at that time, but a few years later did complete the VSV training and has done some support work since.

Ben and Brenda say they stay committed to MADD because they have experienced firsthand the kindness and caring that MADD extends to those in need. They also believe that the more voices there are speaking against drinking and driving, the more likely it is that the laws will change, that their tragedy will not be someone else's tomorrow.

They have over time filled their lives with activities that give them some satisfaction, but life will never be the same as it was before the crash—either crash. When they lost their children and grandson, they lost their dreams, their joy, and their hopes for the future. They have empty spaces in their days that were once filled with their children's presence.

They keep moving forward because they know they have no option. And by sharing their story, they are making a difference in the lives of others. Brenda volunteers with new victims in her area. She helps others because she understands what a new victim's loss feels like, while also acknowledging that no one's loss will feel exactly the same as hers. Each and every situation is different, and we grieve as differently as we love.

But Brenda and Ben don't yet appreciate how much of an effect they are having on other people. How many others have they helped through the maze of grief? How many victims has Brenda sat in court with to support when it seems like no one else does? How many times has she answered the phone to a tearful voice asking for a few moments of time?

I can't imagine how the Wrights have carried on after such a profound and total loss. So much of my own healing has come about because of the little bodies in my life, my grandchildren. In the months that followed Bruce's death, my five-year-old grandson, Austin, would often come to me during a sad moment, put his arms around my neck, and give me a big hug. "Are you missing Bruce?" he'd say. Children know what to do.

And now, without having that support from her own children, Brenda is giving it to others: Listening, caring, giving hugs, and sharing. Making this world a better place.

CHAPTER 11

Honouring Her Spirit

"Ever feel an angel's breath in the gentle breeze? A teardrop in the falling rain? Hear a whisper amongst the rustle of leaves? Or been kissed by a lonesome snowflake? Nature is an angel's favorite hiding place..."

When I think of these words, by Carrie Latet, I think of Bonnie.

Sharon Duffy was adopted, and when as an adult she finally found her birth family, six-year-old Bonnie, her niece, sent Sharon a welcome-to-the-family letter with carefully penned words and pictures that Sharon still treasures. At family birthdays, holidays, and gatherings, Bonnie always came up to Sharon with a hug, the slow, warm kind that makes you feel really loved and special.

Bonnie was Sharon's birth sister's child, but was raised from infancy by Sharon's birth mother, Sylvia, and her mother's partner, James. To Bonnie they were her parents, Mom and Dad. At first Sharon was a little jealous of Bonnie—after all, she was being raised by this wonderful couple, something that Sharon had missed out on until later in life. Sharon was always the quiet one and Bonnie was the baby sister everyone wanted to be around. It wasn't her fault; like moths to a flame, everyone was drawn to Bonnie, young and old. Bonnie always had time for people.

Bonnie loved animals, especially horses and dogs, and her parents would sometimes take her to the rodeo. She loved to ride at home and usually entered the barrel-racing competitions. One day Bonnie shocked everyone when she entered the steer riding as well. I can't imagine the fright she gave her family.

As Bonnie grew up, her life was full of activity. She played hockey, baseball, and much more as a teenager. She even took a rafting trip down the Fraser River in British Columbia. The ten-day adventure was a life-changing experience for Bonnie, and although it wasn't the first time she had been on the river, that particular journey brought her peace and helped develop her leadership skills.

In the autumn of 2007, at the age of eighteen, Bonnie was a beautiful young woman who should have had an exciting future ahead of her.

But on October 13, everything changed. Sharon was at home when Sylvia called and with urgency in her voice told Sharon to come right over. A cold fear went through Sharon as she quickly gathered her things and told her son and husband where she was going.

She knew something was wrong. Her birth mother's house was only a few minutes away, but the trip felt like hours. When Sharon finally arrived she saw that her grandparents were there already.

Sylvia was sitting on the couch and with great distress told Sharon that there had been an accident, and that some of Bonnie's friends thought that she might have been involved.

"What do you mean, *might* have been there?" Sharon asked.

Her mother told her that there had been a terrible car crash, that five young people were in the vehicle, and that the RCMP could not yet say who was involved.

When she heard that there was a possibility that Bonnie was in the crash, Sharon stopped breathing, and over the next few days, she kept finding herself holding her breath as though she could somehow stop time, stop the pain.

Bonnie's involvement was still a rumour, and so to get more information, Sharon drove to the RCMP detachment office. The officers shared only the bare facts: that a bad crash had caused a fire and that seven people were involved. Two had been badly injured and were in critical condition; five young people had been burned to death in the second vehicle.

The crash was so violent that none of the five bodies could be identified, so the RCMP asked them to provide a DNA sample. Sharon returned to the house, pulled some hair from Bonnie's brush, and dropped it off for analysis.

Sharon has a large extended family that lives all over the place, and there were so many people to inform about this tragic crash. Everyone wanted to know the details, but all Sharon could say was that there had been a car crash and that Bonnie may have been killed.

There were a few witnesses to the crash, and finally, by piecing everyone's accounts together, Sharon's family couldn't help but come to the terrible, horrific conclusion that their beloved, joyful, free-spirited Bonnie was gone. It was so hard to believe, especially because they were not able to actually see her, but as time passed, the initial numbness lessened and the pain deepened. They were living something that not one of them could have imagined.

DNA testing takes much longer than it appears to on thirty-minute television shows. A week after the crash, the community held a memorial service without the individual victims even having been confirmed yet.

Over five hundred people came to remember and mourn in their community church. Many family members lived far away and couldn't be there. Others wouldn't attend, refusing to believe that their loved ones were gone. Still others, like Sharon's daughter Brandi, came to the church but were overcome with grief, unable to face the large photos of the five young people thought to be the victims and see the grief on the faces of their friends and family.

Sharon has four children, and it broke her heart to see the pain that they all endured during this time. Three were older than Bonnie and one was younger, and they were all very close. Each child had their own special memories of their time with Bonnie.

Bonnie was their cousin, their friend, and sometimes their confidante. As a parent, Sharon wished her children didn't have to go through the terrible pain of loss. But death is a part of life, and although we try to protect our children from the realities of the world, we can't shelter them forever. But this crash was particularly horrifying because it was so unnecessary, and because the bodies were unidentifiable except by DNA.

It's one thing to look at the remains of someone you love and say goodbye, but to not even be able to see the body, to have your imagination run wild imagining a loved one's last moments, must be so much worse. *Did she cry for help? Did she feel the flames? Was she afraid?* Those are the questions that continue to haunt Sharon's dreams.

The funeral couldn't take place until Bonnie's remains were returned to her family with a positive identification, although it was assumed that she had died, since she was known to have been with those in the car. This didn't happen for a month, and during that time came the news that the driver of the vehicle responsible for the crash had been impaired. It was another blow for the community and the families of the victims. These deaths were no accident. The waste of life could have been prevented!

Those days spent waiting were horrible. It seemed that the community was in limbo, waiting for that degree of closure that burial brings. Finally, Bonnie was laid to rest, near her aunt's house and the horses that she loved, on November 17, 2007, more than a month after the crash that claimed her life.

Sharon has a strong faith and believes that although Bonnie is gone her story is not finished. Her memory will live on in those she left behind. That memory will spur them on to face challenges, give them strength when they feel weak, and give them courage to try something new. The void that Bonnie has left must now be filled with stories about her, and in those stories her spirit will live on and never be forgotten. Her death left a fresh wound and still leaves a huge scar and an ache that will be felt in her family's hearts forever.

After Bonnie's crash, Sharon contacted Gloria Appleby and found in her a warm, caring soul. Gloria helped to bring some sanity back into Sharon's life when she felt that no one understood her or the indescribable pain that she was feeling.

A member of First Nations community in Williams Lake, Sharon works at a First Nations treatment centre. She is very aware of the harmful effects of alcohol on a person, their family, and community, and feels that impaired driving is one of the most unnecessary tragedies.

Sharon came to MADD in Williams Lake when she heard that a new chapter was being formed. She had read about MADD back in the nineties in a *Reader's Digest* article and knew their objective of raising awareness about drinking and driving. She also realized that MADD was trying to educate the public so that no one needed to die so senselessly. She joined the newly founded chapter and soon was busy making a difference in her own community. She helped with their first Project Red Ribbon launch and started setting up information booths at public venues. She feels honoured to be able to do this work.

In 2009, the chapter applied to MADD Canada's special project fund for a grant to create a memorial garden. They considered this a vitally important project because of the sheer number of victims in the area. A memorial garden would be a place for those victim families and loved ones, a place where they could honour the ones they loved. It would not only be a special place to go and remember but would serve as a reminder to others in the community of the dangers of impaired driving. Their application was approved.

The garden was an enormous project, but Sharon feels that if it has helped just one person or one family it will have been worth the chapter's efforts. The beautiful garden also serves as the gathering point for that chapter's annual walk in remembrance of victims.

In 2009 Sharon was invited to attend the Victims' Weekend and Candlelight Vigil in Ontario. It had been eighteen months since Bonnie had died in the crash.

It was a moving experience for Sharon. It was very hard to see the number of people affected by impaired driving, but it was also an opportunity for Sharon to share memories, tell her story, and listen to others. As others too have said, she noticed how the delegates seemed to find comfort there. They shared an experience of losing someone because of impaired driving or being harmed themselves. She noted that even though each tragic experience is different, victims experience similar feelings of shock, disbelief, anger, and overwhelming sadness. Sharon saw other people coming to the same realization she had: They were not alone in their feelings, and they were in a place where people would listen to them and care.

Sharon had another big realization at the conference: Even though she was there because of Bonnie, she was a victim herself via another crash.

In 2001, Sharon was driving with three friends and was hit by a drunk driver. Fortunately, none of them were seriously injured, but two joggers on the sidewalk were also hit, and one of them died soon after. The shock of the crash was horrible. The impaired driver was taken into custody and Sharon had to go to court to testify against him. She wishes that MADD had been in the area then; she could have used the support and might not have felt so alone.

After the crash she wrote to the newspaper trying to describe her feelings. She finished the article by saying that she was not a victim but a survivor; she refuses to allow the fear of another crash consume her.

The impaired driver did serve some time for his criminal actions, but it could never be enough for the family of the man who was killed. And of course it didn't give Sharon back her car, or stop her nightmares.

After the victims' weekend, Sharon decided to become a VSV and help others as she had been helped. There was training being offered in Edmonton, so she went to learn what she could do. It's not an easy job, but being there for victims is the very core of MADD's mission; individual chapters pay to have VSVs trained to help those in their area. Sharon came from the sessions with a new knowledge and the hope that she will never need to use it. The other trainees have become her friends and she can count on them for support at any time.

The training has even helped her when she speaks with her own children and other family members. Every day is a challenge as they continue to work through their loss and live their lives without Bonnie.

Sharon wants to do more to prevent impaired driving in her First Nations community. So much more needs to be done to educate youth in many of the First Nations communities across the country. Crashes in First Nations communities are five times more likely to involve alcohol than in the rest of Canada's population.

Targeting the anti-impaired driving message to youth on the reserve is exactly what needs to be done to decrease these numbers. In 2008, MADD Canada, in conjunction with Bearpaw Media Productions and the Alberta solicitor general, released a video called *Honouring Our Spirit*. It is being used in First Nations communities across the country and is a valuable tool in the battle to keep Aboriginal youth alive.

Sharon sometimes gets frustrated with her MADD chapter, because it doesn't seem to her that they are doing enough. MADD Canada is a volunteer-based organization and each volunteer necessarily brings a different level of commitment to the organization. Yet they have one common purpose, and that is to provide education in regards to impaired driving and to support victims of this violent crime. Sharon has made it her goal to work with her chapter and be involved in special projects such as their memorial garden. She honours Bonnie every day with the work she does and is changing attitudes by educating youth and helping victims.

In her own life, Sharon says that she will continue to learn, to enjoy her family, to be physically active, and to enjoy life as much as she can. That's the example Bonnie set for her.

* * *

Probably one of the most memorable days I spent as national president was in the Aggazi First Nations community near Chilliwack, BC. A local chapter was bringing the new multimedia show "Friday Night" to the school in conjunction with their Project Red Ribbon launch. Local volunteers, police, and paramedics had arranged a mock car crash as well, and five local First Nations communities were bussed to our location at Seabird Island School.

Many elders from the community attended, as well as some of the parents. I shared my story of Bruce with them and the students were very considerate and respectful. After lunch I had the opportunity to chat with many of the youth and I was proud to be part of a ceremony honouring a police officer from the community who had received MADD Canada's regional award for excellence in policing. To see the whole community honour this young officer and perform a blanket ceremony was amazing. Each person joined a circle and embraced the officer in a show of respect, family, and community. Later they brought all of their youth to the front of the room and recognized their importance to the community as well. Each was embraced by everyone present in a continuous circle. I felt so privileged to be able to experience this and later was presented with the ceremonial blanket. It is something I will value always.

But even more I will value the lessons I learned that day: the sense of community, the respect shown for the elders and their wisdom, and hope for the future in their youth.

CHAPTER 12

Kelly's Boys

Kelly Brook had always wanted to be a mother. In 1984, when she was twenty-six, her son Stephen was born. There is always something very special about the birth of your first child. It has nothing to do with loving them more than the others—in one miraculous moment, Kelly had become what she had always wanted to be. Suddenly she became aware that this tiny human being placed in her care was totally dependant on her for everything. Not just love, support, and protection, but even the basic needs of survival. With giving birth, everything changed for her. She never could have imagined the depth of her love for this child, and the need that she felt to protect him.

Kelly and Stephen immediately had a special bond. She couldn't stay away from the hospital nursery. In those days babies were kept in a separate room to give the new mothers a chance to rest. She slipped into the nursery in the wee hours of the morning, picking up her new son in the dimly lit room, rocking and singing to him as he slept.

On the third night, as she sat alone in the quiet room, feeling peaceful and blessed, a nurse entered and told Kelly that she shouldn't be there. She complained that the baby fussed and cried after Kelly left and told her the baby had to learn to sleep on his own. Kelly didn't listen and continued with her nightly visits for the remainder of their stay. She's often thought back to that ridiculous comment.

By the time she was thirty-five, Kelly had four more children. Kevin was born in 1986, Andrew in 1988, Matthew in 1991, and Caitlin in 1992. Kelly says that it never ceased to amaze her, the endless capacity for love and awe she felt when each one of her little darlings was placed in her arms for the first time. They were close in age; Caitlin arrived home just two weeks shy of Stephen's eighth birthday. Having five children under eight years made for a busy home, and Kelly loved every minute of it.

With each passing day, Kelly witnessed the fierce loyalty her children had for one another. She remembers them squabbling as all siblings do, but if anyone outside the family said or did anything against one of them, they were a little army of five, presenting a united front. She loved their loyalty to each other. It was even hard to suppress a smile when they joined forces against *her*.

Kelly lived alone with her children after her marriage ended in 1994. When they were four, six, eight, ten, and twelve, she remarried and was further blessed when her husband brought his daughter, Jenny, to join their family. Jenny had lost her mother to cancer only a few months before and came to live with them. For Jenny it was a new family in a new neighbourhood and she would soon be attending a new school. She was frightened, angry, and grieving for both her mother and her old life.

One day as Kelly held her crying stepdaughter, Jenny swore that she would never get used to the large family and all the noise. Kelly didn't have any experience with grief at that point and found it hard to comfort Jenny and help her other children understand how difficult this new life was for Jenny without her own mother. But she tried.

Several months later, Jenny brought home a friend after school. When the two girls walked in, Jenny's friend looked around, amazed at the number of children, and asked her jokingly how she could stand all the noise. Jenny looked surprised and said that she didn't even notice it. Kelly just smiled.

Halloween was a big event in the Brook household. The kids made creatures and decorations of all kinds. They adorned every window and covered the property. Giant spiders hung from trees, ghosts were propped up on the lawn, pumpkins lined the walkway, and scary music screamed from the entranceway. Kelly always made all the costumes and dressed up with her family. Halloween in 2003 was no exception.

Kelly's son Matthew, twelve that year, was dressed in full chef attire. He looked adorable with his big, puffy chef's hat on his head. His sister, Caitie, had tied a whisk to his sleeve that hung down at his side. It wasn't just a costume for Matthew; he had enjoyed cooking from a young age and even had his own cookbooks. He was allowed to use the school staff room to cook. His teacher realized Matthew's unique passion and wanted to encourage his dream of becoming a great chef.

Early that Halloween night, at about six o'clock, Matthew was walking home from a school Halloween party with five close friends. They were standing at a crosswalk only a few houses from their home. The walkway was brightly lit and filled with children on both sides. Matthew and his friends were standing on a traffic island halfway across the intersection when the light changed, allowing the children to cross. They ran across the intersection and Kelly will always wonder if her son froze in terror or if he even saw the car coming. One of his friends screamed Matthew's name as the rest of them made it across. Matthew was struck by the car and hit the windshield, rolling onto the pavement. The car came to a stop several feet down the road. The whole group witnessed the horror of Kelly's son being hurled through the air.

Kelly was at home when all of this happened. Caitie was just going out the door with a group of friends and their parents. Kevin and Stephen were at work. Andrew and one of his friends, Brent, were home. Kelly received a frantic call from a friend.

She said, "Kelly, come quickly to Shantz Hill, Matt's been hit by a car!"

Brent was standing near Kelly and knew that something was terribly wrong. She grabbed his hand and yelled, "Help me run, Brent, Matt's been hurt!"

Kelly's heart was pounding hard and adrenaline drove her forward. A sickening feeling began to take hold in her stomach, chest, and throat. No matter how hard she ran it didn't seem fast enough, and all the way she kept crying aloud, again and again, pleading with God not to take her baby from her.

When they arrived on the scene, Matthew was on the road being treated by paramedics performing CPR. Kelly wasn't allowed near her child. She wanted to be with him, to whisper words of comfort, to tell him his mommy was there. Police held her back. They told her he was seriously injured and that she needed to stay where she was.

There was a large crowd. Neighbours and people who knew her were all around, trying to support her, telling her that Matt would be all right. Without her knowledge, her fifteen-year-old, Andrew, had followed her and was witnessing this dreadful scene. Somehow, in her heart, Kelly already knew that her son would not survive.

One of Matt's closest friends had stayed until the ambulance arrived. He held Kelly and told her that Matt would be all right, that he had seen him moving, but Kelly knew better. Matt was having a seizure. That was why he was moving.

Matt's blood soaked the pavement. His leg and arm were broken and hemorrhaging. His candy and shoes were strewn across the road. That was the image that was shown on the news the following day—Matthew's candy and his shoes.

All Kelly could think of was that her little boy had been knocked out of his shoes. She felt as though she had been hit in the chest when she saw the image on television.

Friends drove Kelly to Cambridge Hospital. In shock, Kelly behaved calmly and instructed people to bring her children to the hospital. Caitie was still out trick-or-treating and had heard that Matt was injured, but as an eleven-year-old, she thought he'd be okay. She saved her candy to share, knowing that her brother would not be able to go out.

In the emergency room, a police officer came up to Kelly and asked if she was angry. Kelly didn't understand and asked what he meant. The officer told her that the driver had been drinking that night.

Kelly asked if a Breathalyzer test had been done. They said no. She was told that police had smelled alcohol on the driver's breath and when they asked if he had been drinking, he admitted that he had had a couple of glasses of wine. She asked why a Breathalyzer test was not done. She didn't understand. The officer told her that they had done a roadside test and interviewed the driver but did not think he was impaired. Kelly was angry and asked the officer to leave the room. No charges were ever laid against the driver.

Kelly phoned family in Toronto and told them Matthew was critically injured and asked that they drive to McMaster Hospital, where he was being transferred She waited with Matthew for the air ambulance but knew from the look in her son's eyes that it was already too late.

By the time she had arrived at McMaster Hospital, Kelly's actions had become robotic. She greeted the many friends who gradually filled the waiting room, smiling and hugging them, thanking them for coming. She delegated tasks and made sure that her other children had someone with them. She called her daughter Jenny, who was attending UBC, and told her Matt was very sick. She asked her to come home immediately. Her husband was on the road. He didn't have a phone and was notified by a message on his truck screen to go home and go to McMaster Hospital for a family emergency. It took him four hours to reach his family.

That night at McMaster was long. Kelly's children stayed at their brother's bedside. Andrew watched the machine that measured the pressure on Matthew's swelling brain and was alarmed that the numbers wouldn't go down.

Kelly couldn't find the words to tell her children that there would be no recovery. She couldn't tell them that their brother was dying. That they could lose a family member was incomprehensible.

Kelly watched as the doctors performed the tests for brain death. They ran a thread over Matthew's eyes. His pupils remained fixed on the ceiling. They pulled an instrument along the bottom of his feet. There was no response. They turned off Matt's breathing machine and Kelly watched the clock for the longest ten minutes of her life waiting to see if her son would breathe on his own. She stood still, her eyes not leaving his chest. She prayed that he would breathe. He didn't. The last test was the worst. Doctors filled a cup with ice water and poured it into her son's ears. Kelly watched, increasingly certain that her son, who didn't react, was brain dead.

The doctor came into the waiting room, knelt on the floor before the whole family, and told them that Matthew had not responded as they had hoped and had not survived the night.

Kelly's children began to wail, but she couldn't go to them. She sat, paralyzed, her arms wrapped around herself. It was her mother and sister who helped console her children. The hospital hallway was filled with all those who had come from their hometown to show support. Family, friends, teachers, and more. Matthew's hockey team and coaches. That memory will stay with Kelly forever.

Like us, the Brook family decided to donate their son's organs. How do you explain to a child that his brother is already dead when they are taking him away for surgery? We didn't stay to see that part of it, but Kelly did. She sat outside the operating room with the chaplain and when she saw two men rush out to a medical van with a cooler, she knew the cooler held Matthew's organs. Kelly rushed over and told the men that they were carrying life from her son and urged them to drive safely. I can't imagine the shock on their faces as she reminded them of the source of the donor organs. What Kelly remembers is that the cooler looked just like the one they used for camping.

The long drive back to Cambridge was silent. They entered their home and everything seemed different. Something was missing. They didn't know what to do, where to go. A few days later the police returned the costume that Matthew had been wearing. The once-white apron was now stained with his blood. Kelly sat alone behind their home and burned it.

Kelly's recounting of burning Matt's bloodstained clothing haunts me. There were so many similarities in our experiences. We all handle this grief differently, but so much is still the same. I remember those days of trying so hard to do what Bruce would want and trying to do what was socially acceptable. Kelly was no different.

The family all went to the visitation. Kelly greeted all those who came, smiling, calm, and thanked them for coming. Everyone thought she was doing well. They weren't aware that the real Kelly didn't even know herself. She just functioned. They talked about her grace, her strength. People said the usual well-meaning but wrong things.

"Be strong. Everything happens for a reason. God needed another angel. He's in a better place." Kelly wanted to scream but instead played the role expected of her.

After the first few weeks, people stopped visiting. Kelly understood. Most of us are uncomfortable with grief. Only her very close friends and family remained constant. They supported her with their love and listened without giving advice. They allowed her to cry.

Kelly's family tried to begin a new life without their precious Matthew. Grief came in many different forms for all of them. They suffered from post-traumatic stress disorder, anxiety, depression, and nightmares. Daily, Kelly watched her children deteriorate. School wasn't important anymore. Their grades fell.

Kelly still couldn't understand why a Breathalyzer test wasn't done and questioned police continually until they told her that it was too late to do anything.

Finally, one day, alone in the house and overcome with despair, she picked up the phone and called MADD Canada. With the first hello from Gloria, Kelly broke down and sobbed. "My little boy is dead. The driver was drinking. I don't know what to do. I can't live without him."

She didn't know what MADD did but hoped that they could help her. She doubted that anything could ease her pain. What she received was incredible kindness and support. For two hours she poured her heart out, never once questioning whether Gloria had the time to listen. There was no hurry, only patience. Gloria was someone who understood her anger and pain. She couldn't give Kelly what she really wanted, her son home and well, but she cared and allowed her to tell her story.

Maya Angelou writes, "There is no greater agony than bearing an untold story inside of you." How very true that was for Kelly. Many times during that first year she called MADD Canada, just to talk to someone. Gloria was never too busy for her. All she wanted to do was help Kelly until she could help herself.

Kelly felt a multitude of emotions around Matthew's death: loneliness, isolation, anger, longing, despair, helplessness, emptiness, resentment, vulnerability, exhaustion, indecisiveness, and horrendous guilt. But the hardest thing for Kelly was the never-ending feeling of grief. She lost all hope for the future and lived in the darkness that death brings. She thought it would never end. Seeing her children suffer, their innocence shattered, was terrible. The world had become an unfair place for them. They no longer enjoyed the carefree lives of their friends. But as the days, months, and years passed, they began to join the world again. It took a long time for Kelly to feel hope, but over time she began to smile and look at life with a little more optimism.

Kelly decided to go back to work and looked forward to a career and the future. Her children had been through the worst experience of their young lives and were beginning to recover. They weren't the same people they had been before Matt's death, but had become more compassionate and understanding. She was so proud of them and their resilience. It was time for all of them to move on. Life was waiting.

But on November 23, 2007, just after three in the morning, a knock came to Kelly's front door. Two Waterloo regional police officers entered her home. Kelly wasn't afraid at first because she was still sleepy and couldn't imagine what they could want.

The officer said, "Kelly, there's been a very serious car accident, and we believe Kevin has died."

Kelly screamed at her, "No, no, don't tell me that! Don't tell me that, I've already lost a child!"

"I know, Kelly, we know about Matthew, I'm sorry," she said quietly.

Kelly pushed her and hit her on the arm. The officer stood there and didn't move a muscle.

The officer said, "I'm sorry, Kelly."

She asked if they were sure and ran to Kevin's room in the hope that she'd find him asleep in his bed. He wasn't there. Kelly began to shake and feel sick. How could this be happening again?

Maybe they're wrong, she thought to herself. She asked them to describe what Kevin was wearing, and then she knew.

It's funny the way memory works. The routine things you forget. Since the death of her children, Kelly has trouble focusing and remembering many things. Sometimes she will go to change a load of laundry and forget what she's doing when she's halfway down the hall. Kelly says this happens every day in small ways.

But there are some things a person never forgets: Moments of extreme joy, like the days her children were put in her arms for the first time, and moments of extreme horror—the days they were ripped out of them.

Kelly cried and cried, "No, God, no, not again, God, no, I can't do this again!"

By then, Andrew and Caitlin had been woken up and were standing in the hallway, quiet and unmoving, watching the scene unfolding in their home. Without any useless attempts to soften the news, Kelly told them that Kevin had been killed. They didn't speak or utter a sound. Her children just stood there, veterans of horror.

They were taken to Cambridge Hospital by police and Kelly hurried to the basement to view yet another one of her children lying dead in a morgue. Blood had come out of Kevin's ears and his head was misshapen and elongated. One clear blue eye looked at Kelly. She gently closed it. She asked for a washcloth and bowl of warm water so that she could clean the blood from his face, his ears, his neck, and from his teeth. She lay across her son, holding him, crying for her baby. Even though he was a man, 6'1" tall, he was her baby.

Kelly went back upstairs and spoke to police. They told her that the driver, whose car Kevin had been in, was being treated for minor injuries and had just been charged with impaired driving causing death. She was later charged with driving with blood alcohol content of over 0.08 percent and criminal negligence causing death.

Caitlin and Andrew went down to the morgue together, without Kelly; they wanted to be alone when they saw their brother. Kelly says that there is no comfort a mother can provide her children for this. They walked arm in arm to see another brother lying dead from sudden, horrific trauma.

Her son Stephen arrived shortly after, devastated and shaking. Her daughter Jenny arrived fifteen hours later, after arranging yet another flight from Vancouver to bury a brother.

That fragile bit of hope for their future the family had reclaimed disappeared. Once again—twice in only four years—they were burying a family member. Once again they walked zombie-like to their car and made that unbearable, silent journey home.

Kelly felt like she was abandoning her son. He should have been coming home with them. He would never come home again. It was a staggering blow to enter his room, to sit on the bed and feel the emptiness all around her.

The days before the funeral were a blur of angry outbursts, screaming, crying, shock, agony, and disbelief. Once again, at the visitation and the funeral the family assumed the expected of the bereaved. They greeted and thanked mourners with dignity, maintaining control, keeping emotions in check. Underneath the dulling numbness they wanted to scream. These people were only there for a short while and would return to their safe homes, and Kelly's family would be left with a void. Only a special few of their friends would remain close— the kind of friends you can call in the pre-dawn hours, when the night is the darkest, when you believe you are going crazy and cannot survive another minute.

The services were over, but the investigation continued. Kelly was living alone with her children again after her second marriage had ended that year. She was left to deal regularly with police, the crown attorney's office, the victim assistance worker, and the Alcohol and Gaming Commission. She also had to navigate insurance claims for her disability, discussions with her lawyer for a civil suit, and court appearances. Then there was continual contact with her children's schools, and the family's doctors' and counsellors' appointments. There was financial stress from loss of income, and in February of 2008, she lost her job. She just couldn't go back.

And all because someone had decided to drive drunk and had killed her son.

The driver's blood alcohol content was .239—almost three times the legal limit. Kevin had recently met her at work. They were friends. Kelly had told the officer at the house that it was impossible that Kevin would get in a car with a drunk driver. She told the officer that she was always available for her children, that she picked them up at any hour with no questions asked. She always left cab money in the kitchen.

Kevin had called for a taxi that night. He knew his friend was too drunk to drive. When police returned Kevin's cellphone, after cleaning off his blood, Andrew and Kelly found the call made to the Cambridge taxi company.

But the offender refused to get into the cab. She argued for so long, the cab driver left. She quarrelled with bar staff, screaming and swearing, while Kevin apologized for her behaviour. They began to walk the short distance home, but she was still determined to drive and doubled back and for the third time got behind the wheel. For more than an hour, bar staff tried to control the situation themselves instead of calling police.

In the end the bar was given a forty-five-day suspension. They were found responsible for allowing the driver to become so drunk that she was more than three-and-a-half times the legal limit. By the time the bar called 911 it was too late. Kevin died less than a kilometre down the road when the car crashed into a concrete power pole.

That night Kevin had two choices: take the cab by himself and watch that girl drive home, or get in the car with her to see that she found her way. He made the wrong decision and it cost him his life. The price for his mistake was too high.

During one of her meetings with the crown attorney, Kelly asked if she could see the photos of the crash scene. She felt a duty to her son to know what had happened.

It was hard to see her child lying on the gravel. His shirt and jacket were pulled up after he was removed from the car. His face and clothing were covered in blood, his skin exposed to the cold November air. Kelly was sick, not just with horror at the crash scene, but at the lack of dignity for Kevin. It was so offensive to see the son she had cared for lying beside the wreckage of the car.

Kevin's feet were crossed, just as if he were lying on the couch.

She looked at his clothes in the picture and remarked to Mr. Townsend, the crown prosecutor, "We were able to have his jacket cleaned, but I burned those clothes in my backyard. I couldn't put them out with the trash—they weren't garbage. On two separate, cold November days, I've sat before a fire in my backyard and burned my children's bloody clothing."

"You paid homage," he said softly.

The family saw pictures of the crash in the paper, the way they did after Matthew's death. It was exceptionally hard looking at the photos and imagining what had happened that night. They also read what the ambulance driver said—that he couldn't smell the alcohol on the driver's breath because the smell of Kevin's blood was overwhelming. The drunk driver walked away with only a minor injury and bruising.

The worst for Kelly were the pictures that she saw later on Facebook. They showed the impaired driver laughing, drinking, and posing for the camera. At the end of the day, she received only a thirty-month sentence. Kevin is dead, and Kelly's family has been sentenced to a lifetime of missing him.

Kelly told me that during this time they received remarkable support at many levels. Their crown attorney was kind and compassionate and kept them well informed. The police came to their home on countless occasions to answer questions, always with the utmost respect. The victim assistance worker was incredibly supportive through every court appearance.

But the agony that had once consumed Kelly had returned with a vengeance. Her children were inconsolable. PTSD had become chronic for them all and their grief, now labelled "complicated grief," was accompanied by a general fear so overwhelming that nothing helped, certainly not sleep.

Again they fell into that black hole that had been their companion for so long. Since Matthew's death they had been cautious and scared, but they had finally allowed themselves to believe this could never happen again. They believed, but they were wrong.

Kelly remembered the help she had received from MADD Canada a short time before and again called Gloria. She told her that she had lost another son and Gloria responded.

"Is this Kelly? Oh, Kelly, we heard, we were devastated and shocked by the news. We're all so sorry."

Once again Kelly cried her heart out to this woman who had given her comfort just four years before. After everything they had been through together, the two women had never yet met.

But this time was different. Kelly was beyond angry—she was enraged, and felt it was time to fight back. MADD had helped her when Matthew died, and this time she was determined to help MADD Canada.

She contacted the television show W5 and told them her story. They filmed the episode "To Serve or Protect," which focuses on the responsibility of licensed establishments and their service of alcohol. She met with Alcohol and Gaming Commission CEO Jean Major and MADD Canada CEO Andy Murie.

Kelly wanted to do anything she could to bring more attention to this devastating, costly, violent crime that kills and maims and injures so many Canadians. She spoke to liquor license inspectors at seminars and at workshops for many policing agencies. She met with Ontario Provincial Police Commissioner Julian Fantino to ask for his help.

She participated in the making of a Reduce Impaired Driving Everywhere (RIDE) training video with the Niagara Regional Police and looks forward to speaking at the next meeting of the Canadian Association of Chiefs of Police to tell her story and lend motivation and support.

Kelly is committed to speaking to high schools and grade eight students in the Cambridge area, and opening the MADD multimedia presentations. She has completed a course with Victim Services of Waterloo Regional Police and is an on-call crisis responder. She wants to help others as she was helped.

She attended her first national victims' weekend in 2010 and her experience mirrors so many others. She marvelled at the organization and dedication of the staff that made sure that each victim was treated with care and compassion. She felt like part of a larger family. Kelly's pain was validated and accepted and she didn't want to leave. She felt a kinship with people she had just met for the first time. And her most revealing statement is that she can't wait to attend another weekend. It was great to hear her talk about the future in a good way. Kelly says that she has never felt so truly understood by so many people at one time, in one place.

Kelly has had six years to reflect on Matthew's death and two years to reflect on Kevin's. She has become an expert in a field she wanted to know nothing about. Her lessons can serve to help us all understand.

She says that that's one of the hard things about death. Other people who have not lost often cannot understand why you don't go back to work, or school; why it is so hard to share your feelings; why you can't simply "move on" and "rejoin the world of the living." Grief doesn't work that way. It's lifelong. What time limit could we possibly place around caring about the people we've lost? When spring comes, it comes without your son, your brother, your wife, your mother. It is a lonely world for the grieving heart.

Kelly adds that her heart will always ache for her boys. Her sense of safety is gone. She will never forget the images of her dead children—of the car flattened down to the seat by a cement hydro pole where Kevin had been sitting, and of Matthew dying on a cold road surrounded by his young friends.

She wonders if Kevin and Matthew felt, for even one second, terror before they lost their lives. Kelly says that she can't bear to visit those thoughts, but they visit her.

She wonders if this kind of damage to her surviving children can ever be healed. She knows as their mother that they are profoundly changed and that they will carry this pain in their hearts till the end of their days.

Grief changes everyone involved. MADD Youth is a place for young people, like Kelly's children, who have lost family or been injured themselves. It's someplace they can feel normal, whatever normal means to them now. They can learn to grieve by sharing their pain and frustration and they have the ability to reach out to their peers and change attitudes. They can help save or change lives.

Kelly tries to honour Kevin and Matthew by allowing her heart to be open to life, love, and hope. She feels a powerful light from within and a strength that comes from something stronger than her. She feels that the death of a child can break you and make you lose sight of the beauty of life, or it can help you see that beauty in a clearer light. She's looking for the beauty.

Kelly found this quote from George Eliot that describes what she feels:

"There is no despair so absolute as that which comes with the first moments of our first great sorrow, when we have not yet known what it is to have suffered and be healed, to have despaired and have recovered hope."

She has known the despair, the sorrow, and the recovered hope, not once but twice. She went back to work, but it's not enough anymore—

her tolerance level for the mundane is gone. She hopes to become a motivational speaker.

Her experiences have made her an expert and she knows she can help others, which gives her a sense of purpose—as does her family. That's a good thing. Life is worth living and living well.

* * *

It seems like we are losing so many of our young people. Research says that youth are overrepresented in deaths and injuries on our highways, both as victims and drivers. Although there has been a significant decline in road fatality and injury rates among teens over the last two decades, progress in the recent past has stalled. Road crashes still remain the leading cause of death among teenagers and more nineteen-year-olds die or are seriously injured in these crashes than any other age group.

The main reasons are inexperience and immaturity. Forty-five percent of those who are killed in road crashes have been drinking, and although more and more teenagers are getting the message, those who still drink and drive run a very high risk of being in a collision. Most of the dead or injured teens are young men, and more crashes tend to happen in the summer or on weekends. Most die at night and are the impaired drivers.

By the time a young driver has a blood alcohol limit of 0.10 percent, just above the legal limit of 0.08 percent, he or she is *fifty-one times* more likely to be involved in a crash than a non-drinking young driver. In many of the courts this has been described as "minimal intoxication" and often police won't even charge until the driver is at this level. It is any wonder that MADD Canada members are advocating for increased suspensions at 0.05?

As part of the Rating the Provinces report card, MADD Canada has asked all provinces to have graduated licensing systems in place and zero tolerance for alcohol for the first five years of driving. This brings our youth generally to the age of twenty-one before the can legally drive after drinking. In many cases it will set a standard that will continue the rest of their lives. Regardless, if they choose to drink in moderation, keeping their blood alcohol content below the legal limit, after the first five years they will have become more experienced drivers and will be less likely to be involved in crashes. The new drinker/new driver combination is, as we are all too aware, deadly.

That's why it is so important for MADD volunteers and especially victims to tell their stories whenever possible. I've shared Bruce's story many times, but perhaps the most effective and memorable time was at a presentation I did at an Antigonish high school in the spring of 2007. I had a call from the local MADD Antigonish chapter president, Kyla, asking if I could come to a mock crash for the graduating class. They were asking me to speak after the crash. She also told me that a police officer would be there. That was nothing out of the ordinary, but, she added, "He was one of the officers at Bruce's crash."

I paused, shocked by what she had said but determined that I could still do the job. I told her I'd be there and decided that I wouldn't talk to the officer until after the presentation and then if I needed to I could cry.

A few days later I drove into the schoolyard ready for the presentation. Constable Bryce Haight introduced himself to me immediately. He said that he had been waiting to meet me and wanted to let me know how sorry he was about Bruce's death. I thanked him and asked if we could speak later.

The mock crash was well done, with firefighters and police from the local area making it look very real. The students were visibly impacted by the display, and especially by seeing some of their friends made up as victims and covered in blood. Then we all headed into the school theatre for the speakers. What I didn't know that day was that Bryce would be speaking before me. And his topic was Bruce's crash.

He walked onto the recessed stage with hundreds of students watching. Joining the students were the firefighters and police who had helped with the mock crash, and some of the local media. A large crate was centre stage, just perfect for sitting. He took off his hat and sat. You could see the emotion in his face as he began. Bryce had started his policing career as an auxiliary offer in Montague, PEI, just a few minutes from Caledonia. They were at a coffee shop that night when they had a call about a collision. Usually that's not a real concern. Fender benders are pretty common. It was a rainy night and they started toward Caledonia, the scene of the reported crash. He said it was the strangest thing. Just before they got there the rain stopped. It was as if the whole scene was in a bubble. He described the vehicles and a lifeless form on the roadside. He heard the voice of one of the victims in the truck calling for help. He saw the hunting dogs running down the road and the other hunters, Bruce's friends, around the vehicles. The setting was surreal. He described the crunch of the debris under his feet as he walked around the crash scene. It was his job to block the road to make sure that no one came over the hill and found themselves in the middle of all of this.

By this point in his speech I was standing there, tears steaming down my face, trying not to listen too much, trying to stay composed. It was impossible.

Bryce came back to the scene a little later, after Bruce and Jason had been taken by ambulance to the hospital. He had heard by then that Bruce was a police officer, and the news stunned him. He told the students about going home to his wife that night, sitting on the bed, and only being able to relive that scene over and over again. Bryce's tears flowed as he told his story.

Then he talked about how he had wanted to meet Bruce's mother and how he had been on the MADD Canada website and saw what we were doing in his memory.

That's when he introduced me. We shared a hug as he left the stage and I took his place, sitting on that crate. I don't think my legs would have held me. My first words were, "And that's where my story starts." My notes fell to the floor, forgotten as I told them about Bruce, his hopes and dreams and all that we had lost. I told them about that day and night and made them feel our loss. There wasn't a dry eye in the house. Those stoic firefighters wiped their tears and the students were a mess. That poor reporter couldn't even take notes. I talked about Bruce and I talked about the drunk driver and what he too had lost because of his actions.

Those students will never forget that presentation and neither will I. I left Antigonish drained physically and mentally, but feeling oddly victorious.

Since then Bryce and I have met at other school events and again we share that night, but never with the same level of emotion and pain. Each time he speaks I'm back there with Bruce and each time I learn a little more about that fateful night.

CHAPTER 13

The Legacy

Since Bruce's death I've been more watchful, more aware, when I hear about car crashes on the news. If alcohol is not a factor, I'm always relieved—although I still feel for any family who has suffered a loss. The pain of any unnecessary death or injury is debilitating. But when alcohol is involved, it becomes personal.

In the fall of 2006, I saw a news story about a young New Brunswick couple that had been killed in a crash. Their children were in the car with them and one was also badly hurt. When the drunk driver went to court his lawyer made a comment that incited rage in Canadians everywhere. His statement—which you will find in the story below— became a catalyst for many to make change.

The following spring at the National Victims' Weekend and Candlelight Vigil of Hope and Remembrance, I met Rick and Sue McNulty. Their daughter, Laura, and son-in-law, Greg, were the victims of that crash, and now they were raising their grandchildren, Kali and Jeremy. Jeremy was the child who had been badly injured, and he was still suffering from those injuries, but the biggest issue the children had to deal with was the loss of their parents. At the next national victims' weekend, in 2008, I had the opportunity to meet the kids. They are such a sweet pair. Jeremy is a typical young boy— growing too fast and trying to fit in. The problem is that he will always be different because of his experiences. He has experienced so much pain and loss in his young life.

And then there is Kali—willowy, beautiful, and too wise for her years. We've become even closer over the years and just lately she has started to talk about her feelings and that night that robbed them of their parents.

Their story begins on October 29, 2006, two days before Halloween. Every year Greg and Laura would take Kali, twelve that year, and Jeremy, nine, dressed in their Halloween costumes, to see Greg's parents and grandmother, who lived in Saint John about thirty minutes away from their home in Hampton. This was a family outing they looked forward to and loved; that year was no exception. Kali and Jeremy's Nan had given them maple fudge as a treat that year, along with lots of chocolate cake.

They were a very happy family most of the time. Kali says that sometimes they would fight or there would be arguments, but that's inevitable. She says that "perfect" families who don't fight once in a while just don't care about each other. She and her mother loved each other, and sometimes they did argue, but they didn't yell. Their battles were silent. Kali wonders if that would have changed had they been given the chance to have a future together. She'll never know.

The family was getting along really well that night and having fun. They had to leave Saint John early, though, because Jeremy had a hockey game back home. Laura dug out her cellphone and called her mother, who had been planning to join them for the game. The hockey game had been cancelled and they would be going straight home instead.

It was a rainy and foggy night and she knew that her mother would worry, so Laura promised to call again as soon as they got home. The last words Sue heard from her daughter were, "I love you, Mom." Sue answered, "I love you too." Saying those last words to her daughter would come to mean more to her than anyone can imagine.

Kali didn't feel good about the drive. Something was wrong. Kali couldn't exactly say what, but the feeling in her gut wouldn't get better. She worried that it was related to a recurring nightmare she'd had since she was little: that she saw two cars collide, and then heard screaming. In the nightmare there were flames and smoke and her parents, clearly in the car, died. Everyone in the car died.

That night looked and felt so similar to the atmosphere in her nightmare that Kali knew something bad was going to happen. They were all pretty quiet on the way home, and when she looks back on the night she wonders if everyone sensed the impending danger. Jeremy dug out a video game and started playing; the light from the screen was bugging her father so he asked Jeremy to dim it. Her parents were talking about weight loss programs and starting a new one. Kali finds that so ironic when she looks back. They were talking about new beginnings when their time was about to end.

The feeling in Kali's stomach was getting worse and worse so she dug out a mirror, lifting it so she could see behind the car. Nothing was coming from behind. She put the mirror away and settled back in her seat. She checked the clock. Kali had just barely glanced away from the clock when she saw bright lights speeding towards them. She didn't tense up and freeze like Jeremy, but instead leaned back, bracing herself for the impact.

The car filled with screaming. The noise was brutal. She'll never be able to forget her mom's terrified cries. Her father was quiet—Kali realized he was gone before the car even stopped spinning. She heard Jeremy screaming, but behind the screams everything was too quiet.

Her head spun. She thought the car was spinning, but really, it was the force of her head hitting the glass. The glass didn't break. It remained intact as the rest of the car was crushed.

When everything stopped spinning and the blackness lifted, Kali saw disaster. She felt like she was seeing her entire life bleeding out in front of her. First she looked at her mom, then her dad. She shook them, pleading with them to wake up. Jeremy writhed beside her, screaming at the top of his lungs. He was in shock from pain and the amount of blood that surrounded him. Jeremy doesn't remember most of the crash, only what Kali's told him.

A family was standing outside and had seen everything. They tried to calm Kali down and told her that help was on the way. Kali yelled and swore at them, terrified by what was happening all around her. She knows that they were only trying to help, but she was so scared.

She turned her attention away from the horror-stricken family and toward her nine-year-old baby brother. Kali says that she's always been closer to Jeremy than anyone else in her life. He's ultimately her baby boy, and she'll never be more scared or hurt than she was thinking she was going to lose him. That's what it looked like. His blood covered her, everywhere. The cooler she had placed in the car earlier that day had snapped his femur in half.

Kali saw the white of his bone sticking out from beneath his black pant leg, and saw the horror in his eyes as he realized what it was he was touching. She moved his hands, and snapped his leg back, putting as much weight on it as she could. Kali doesn't know how she knew that she needed to keep him talking, but somehow she did. Kali told him that everything was going to be okay and that he needed to keep telling their mom that they were fine.

Kali moved enough to pull at the seatbelt that confined her. It was stuck, and she squirmed and pulled. She bruised her neck and waist trying to break free of the belt. She was trying to get to her mom and the cellphone. Something was telling her, "Tell your grandparents to meet you at the hospital."

Thinking back, Kali says that she almost thinks it was her dad whispering in her ear, somehow. She knows her parents wouldn't have left her and Jeremy there to die. Their spirits would have stayed around.

Rick and Sue were at home and had just finished eating when they heard the sirens go by their house. They realized that something must have happened but never dreamed it could have anything to do with them.

Kali continued to try and reach her mother's purse and phone but finally gave up. She started to beat on the window. Again, the family told her to stop, that she'd be fine. But Kali didn't care about herself and would have changed places with any of her family members at that moment, to save them that pain.

She heard the police sirens coming and it seemed that they had arrived in a matter of only seconds—later she found out from one of the officers that they had already been looking for the driver. He had been reported earlier in the evening as a suspected drunk driver.

When the firefighters arrived they freed Kali and asked her to cover her mom and dad. Until Kali shared this story with me, she had forgotten that she was the one who had to cover their faces. Next, she turned and covered her brother and herself. The firefighters then broke the windows to get them all out.

Kali thinks that the firefighters realized they wouldn't be able to save her mother. She was told later that her mother had died on impact, but Kali knows her mother was breathing when Kali left the car.

She realizes that people may have thought her a child, small and in-nocent or even stupid, but she knew how to take a pulse. Her mother was breathing up until the moment Kali left the vehicle and couldn't see her anymore.

The firefighters wanted Kali out of the car, but she refused. She wanted her family out first. They promised her it would be safer for everyone if she left the car. What strikes Kali as really odd is that she walked away from that fatal crash. She stood up from the car, and the only thing that kept her from walking to the ambulance was fear. She was so scared she could barely breathe.

Kali insisted that she call her grandparents before getting into the ambulance. She had to tell them what happened. The officer got Sue on the line and told her that there had been an accident and they had Kali with them and that she wanted to speak to her grandparents.

Sue's first question when Kali came on the line was to ask if she was all right. Kali sounded scared and upset as she told her grandmother that she had hurt her head and arm, but she was okay. Then Sue asked about Jeremy. Kali answered that Jeremy was bleeding really badly. Finally Sue asked about Kali's mom and dad and Kali replied that they were unconscious or something.

Kali asked her grandparents to come to the hospital.

"Okay, sweetie," her grandmother replied. "Papa and I will meet you there."

Kali feels bad about that call. She knows that her grandmother was happy to hear her voice, but it was Kali who gave her the terrible news about the crash.

Rick hastily grabbed their things and together they ran to the car. It was a drive filled with prayers that their worst fears would not be real-ized. That they would find their family battered and bruised but not dead. Sue says that she had never had such a long drive filled with so much terror in her life.

In her heart Sue realized that Greg and Laura were gone, but she couldn't acknowledge it yet in her head. She still had to have hope that everything would be all right.

Finally they arrived at the hospital, but the staff would not let them see anyone; nor would they answer any questions. Instead they were directed to a small room and had to wait for someone to come to them, to give them the answers to the thousand questions in their heads. The RCMP finally came into the room and told them that Greg and Laura had expired at the scene of the crash.

Sue's mind went blank—and all she could think was, "When Laura was born I checked her all over and there was no expiry date, so they must be wrong!"

Sue asked to see her daughter and was advised by the hospital that it would be better not to see her remains. Sue reluctantly agreed at the time but now wishes that she had seen Laura anyway—just to touch a piece of her hair or her hand. Something, anything, just to be sure it was her Laura, and to say goodbye.

Jeremy and Kali never saw their parents again after they were taken from the car. Those last moments of horror and fear will be seared in their memories forever.

Eventually Rick and Sue were allowed to see their grandchildren and talk to the doctor. They were told that Kali was physically in good shape but in shock. Jeremy, on the other hand, had serious injuries. He had two broken legs, a broken neck, a lacerated kidney and liver, a herniated bowel, and a concussion.

Kali had been fading in and out of consciousness between the crash scene and the hospital. She was wearing a neck brace but it hurt her and she didn't like it. She fought the nurses who tried to put her IV in place. It took two of them—one to hold her down, another to hold her arm and shove it in. She remembers her grandmother coming in and sitting beside her, rubbing her leg, promising Kali that it would all be over soon. Kali says that it's the only promise her grandmother has ever broken— for Kali this will never, ever be over. She'll always hurt. She'll never be the old Kali again. Kali talked about that time in the hospital, saying "I'm a new me, a different me, one without parents, without a mother, without my best friend. But I didn't know that yet. I thought Mama was being taken care of. In a way, she was. She was in the morgue."

The man in the next bed moaned and groaned. He'd been in an accident. A head-on collision. His arm was broken and he was drunk. He was the one who killed Kali's parents.

Soon they came to take Jeremy for x-rays. Sue stayed with Kali and Rick went to call everyone, to deliver the news that he hadn't even fully grasped yet. That Greg and Laura were dead and their children were orphans.

Greg and Sue remember that night as the longest of their lives. Kali was on the first floor and Jeremy was in the intensive care unit on the fourth floor. They took turns throughout the night. First Sue would stay with Kali while Rick sat with Jeremy. About every forty-five minutes they would switch.

During the night Greg's mother and father and their families arrived from Saint John. Each solemn greeting and tearful hug reinforced the tragedy that had become their lives.

Kali kept waking up all night. She'd throw up and then fade out again and again. The images of blood, flesh, bones, and the crash were all permanently embedded in her mind.

At one point, Kali woke up for a minute.

"Nana?"

"Yes, baby?"

"Nana, is Jeremy okay?"

"He's fine, baby…"

"What happened?"

"Honey, there was an accident…"

"Mama and Daddy?"

"They went to heaven, baby girl…Mommy and Daddy went to heaven."

A drugged Kali just smiled and nodded—heaven sounded better than what Jeremy was going through. Many thoughts plagued her mind that night. Finally, she realized that she and her brother were now alone. She knew they had lots of relatives and friends, but their family wasn't their family anymore. It would never ever be the same. She remembers worrying about Jeremy, and who would take care of them if not their parents. They had different fathers. What if they were split up? What if she lost her brother?

Early the next morning, Jeremy woke up and his first questions were about Kali and his parents. I can't imagine how much strength it took for Rick to look into his grandson's eyes and tell him that his mother and father were in heaven.

It was as if Jeremy already knew, for he closed his eyes and said, "Who's going to take care of us now?" Rick answered that he and Sue would. Jeremy said "good" and went back to sleep.

Later Jeremy asked Rick if his name would change to McNulty and if he would be calling Rick his dad from now on. Rick told Jeremy that he would always be an O'Dell and then left his grandson. He went out the nurses' station, where the strain caught up with him and he cried for all they had lost.

The next day, meetings started with the doctors. They told Rick and Sue that Kali had probably saved her brother's life by keeping him alert and keeping pressure on his injuries.

Kali was happy to be able to see Jeremy again. She had kept a little food down that morning, so the nurses put her in a wheelchair to go to her brother. She was horrified. It was almost worse seeing him in the light. His legs were wrapped in casts; there was a tube in his nose. He looked so fragile. To her he looked dead. And the fact that he was suffering so much scared Kali even more. She couldn't understand how two people had died, one had come close, and that she had made it through with nothing but bad memories.

Because of his extensive injuries, it was decided that Jeremy needed to be moved to the nearest children's hospital, the IWK in Halifax. Meanwhile the family needed to get through the funeral for Laura and Greg.

Rick, Sue, Kali, and hundreds more said their final goodbyes to Greg and Laura on an early November day with promises of winter in the air. It was not the only promise of the day. Silently Rick and Sue made a pledge to their daughter and son-in-law that they would care for Kali and Jeremy and be there for them in their stead. They promised to try to take care of them the way Laura and Greg would have wished. To see them grow and have a normal upbringing and home life. It's a promise they renew every day.

Finally, the last words of committal were said, and the McNultys began to look ahead. They couldn't do any more for Greg and Laura, but they could for the kids. Jeremy was waiting for them in Halifax, so Rick, Sue, and Kali went down to visit.

Sue couldn't wait to see Jeremy, to touch him and tell him how much she loved him. When she first saw him in his bed he looked so little and broken, but he was so brave. Even with all his pain he smiled, and when he said the word "Nana" it was music to her ears.

Kali and Jeremy were so happy to see each other and to finally know that the other was okay. Jeremy had some really bad days; the hardest one was when they fitted him for his body cast. Sue remembers that Jeremy started to scream that he wanted to die to stop the pain. It just broke her heart and she had to leave the room so she could break down privately without upsetting her grandson.

For a week they took turns at Jeremy's bedside and then finally decided it was time for Sue and Kali to return to their home. Rick decided that he would stay in Halifax until his grandson was able to come home. It didn't matter how long it would take.

The hospital set up a cot for Rick beside Jeremy's bed so he could be there day and night. Rick's worst nights were when Jeremy would cry out in his sleep. The horrific images of the crash that killed Jeremy's parents haunted him.

Of all the horrors of the previous weeks, Rick's worst moment came the day of the offender's first court appearance—news coverage of which I saw myself. That was the day the offender's lawyer said something so outrageous that it was a call to arms for many. On camera, the offender's lawyer said, "People talk on cellphones and kill people, people watch a deer in a field and kill people, and people drink and drive and kill people. It's not going to stop today and it's not going to stop tomorrow so I don't see what the big public outcry is." Rick was sitting at Jeremy's bedside watching his grandson's suffering and was outraged that the drunk driver's lawyer was implying that Jeremy's parents were nothing more than roadkill. Rick was furious and was going crazy. But for now there was nothing he could do.

With Kali and Sue in Salisbury and Jeremy and Rick in Halifax the next while was challenging, but Jeremy was released a week before Christmas and they were finally together again.

That first Christmas was tough. It was too early to smile or have nice memories of Christmases past, and everyone was overly cautious, trying not to say something that would upset anyone else. The kids missed their parents so much. The day finally passed and they could breathe a little easier again.

Jeremy was still far from a full physical recovery. Twice a week they made the trip to Moncton for physiotherapy. Progress was slow; he still had to be carefully lifted in and out of his wheelchair for everything. His only freely moving parts were his arms. The body cast went from the top of his head to just below his waist, and both legs were in casts from top to bottom. It was a long, hard road to recovery.

They also had to deal with all the legalities involved. The most important thing, of course, was the care and custody of the kids. Rick and Sue were happy to take over that responsibility. They only wished there was no need to.

Greg and Laura had bought a house just the year before. It was their first home and they were so proud of it. Now Rick and Sue were left with the task of packing up the house and getting it ready for sale. What made it hard was the knowledge that each and every item was special to Greg and Laura. One after another, each piece brought on a new flood of tears.

Worse yet was the phone line. Rick and Sue would call every hour to hear Laura's voice on her voicemail message. Sue says that the day they had to disconnect the phone, it was like losing Laura all over again.

The next hurdle was the trial of the offender. At first he pleaded not guilty, and selected trial by judge alone. Over the next eighteen months the defense used every delay tactic they could possibly employ.

As time passed, Rick and Sue had the feeling the courts were all about the offender—his rights, court rescheduling, and the restrictions the defense could put on victim impact statements. It was unbelievable that a victim's impact statement had to be approved by the offender!

Rick could not understand why the crown was only asking for seven years when the maximum allowable was life in prison for impaired driving causing death. The crown attorney said that he didn't want to ask for more, so there wouldn't be a chance for an appeal.

The final insult came when the convicted drunk driver was given a parole hearing after only eighteen months in custody. A parole officer told the court that the drunk driver had found Jesus while in prison. He tried to tell the court that the crash had been God's way of making him stop drinking.

Rick was furious. Did that mean that it was okay to kill two people as long as the offender quit drinking? Rick says that this is not the God he knows. The church can teach that God can forgive anything, but Rick's the first to admit that he's not God and he doesn't know if he'll ever be able to forgive that driver.

Rick says that the family's first contact with MADD Canada was a lifesaver. Someone—he can't remember who—slipped him a card with a message saying that if they wished to talk, here was the contact information. So simple, but still a lifeline of hope for the family. It wasn't until after Rick and Jeremy came home from Halifax that they contacted Karen Dunham. She was with the MADD Saint John and Area chapter and had just finished her term as national president. (Karen was my predecessor.)

She gave the family a lot of information that has helped them through some very tough times. There were books on dealing with holidays, information about losing a child, and so much more.

She also prepared them for dealing with the court system, and told Rick and Sue what to expect. And every time the family went to court, Karen Dunham went with them. The McNultys say they might not have been able to deal with the process without her by their side, explaining things each step of the way. Trying to make sense of the senseless.

Rick and Sue decided that when the trial was over and the drunk driver received whatever sentence the court decided, they would volunteer their services to MADD. They would try to help others and make changes in the criminal justice system in whatever small way they could.

After the sentencing, Rick and Sue joined the chapter, where they are making a big difference in their own community.

The last time I talked to Jeremy, he was telling me a joke. He is for the most part pain-free, and it's clear that the tie between him and Kali is stronger than ever.

And Kali, she's doing better as well. For that first year after leaving the hospital, everything was a blur and she was in complete denial.

She was convinced that it was all a cruel joke—that it was all a skit or something she'd been left out of. For a while she let herself believe that her mom had just lost her memory and that she'd get it back and come find them soon. Everything just seemed surreal, like a bad dream. She asked herself why again and again, and then one day realized that if you ask "why me?" for the bad things, then you need to ask it for every blessing as well.

Kali has just recently started speaking about her losses and her experience. She is starting to feel less alone in the world. At her first MADD victims' weekend she met other MADD youth victims and now feels connected to them. Knowing she has that support makes it easier for her to get out of the bed in the morning.

But the experience she's gone through has made high school so much harder. She feels that kids really do take life for granted. She says that she's seen death in all its glory and fear, and it forced her to grow up. She fights, vents, moans, and groans, but she rarely means it. She doesn't see the point in excessive drinking or in drugs or parties. She has learned that life's too short, too bittersweet, to let even the smallest thing slip through your fingers.

Kali still has horrible nightmares, constant headaches, and an empty yearning in her heart. That will never go away. She will always want her parents back. She wants her mother back, if only for a day. She misses her so much and will never have her there for things like graduation, marriage, childbirth—the important things in life. Her kids won't have a grandmother; her future family won't ever know how phenomenal her mom really was. To them, she will always be a memory and nothing more. A face on paper, words on a page, but not a real person. It's always going to sting, and there's nothing anyone can do to change that now.

Kali says that the drunk driver made his choice: he drove under the influence. He cut the string that held her parents here when he turned his keys in the ignition. Their deaths are on his hands, and for that, she almost pities him. He has to live with it for the rest of his life, just as she and Jeremy have to live without parents. But then Kali remembers the difference: she and Jeremy didn't have a choice. The driver did.

Kali has started talking to teenagers at schools about her experience. It takes a lot of bravery to stand before hundreds of people when you're an adult, let alone sixteen. Kali says that it makes her feel good to see the look on students' faces and know that her words are touching them and making them change their attitudes about impaired driving. She had done a public service announcement that airs frequently on New Brunswick television and is on the MADD Canada website. In it she is brutally honest. She is changing attitudes and saving lives.

This amazing family has gone through more than anyone should have to, and they have persevered and are turning the terrible loss of Greg and Laura into a life-changing lesson for everyone. I'm sure that as Kali stands on the stage in front of her peers, or tells their terrible story to someone new, her parents are there by her side. Cheering.

The Gift

In our grief we have one wish, and I know it is shared by many: The desire that our loved one not be forgotten. In our case, after the funeral we had many of Bruce's things that we didn't have a place for—the flag that draped his coffin; his police hat, presented to me at graveside; his cowboy hat, used when competing at the horse shows; his badge, which he carried with such pride; and several other things. I didn't want them put away; I wanted them with me every day. I racked my brain trying to find some way to have them visible, a part of our daily lives. It was important to me that the mementoes of Bruce's life not become dust collectors but be appreciated.

After a long search I found a mantle-style curio that satisfied my requirements perfectly, and I was excited when it was delivered to our home. It had a marble top, intricate carved wood, and curved glass. It was perfect and gave several of Bruce's special things a permanent place.

The cabinet became a part of everyday life for us. Bruce was always with us. Never was this more apparent than a few years later, when I was having a conversation with my four-year-old grandson, Troy, who was born after Bruce's death.

Troy had always been fascinated with the cabinet, and it was not unusual to see him as a toddler carrying Bruce's phone—yes, our own private psychic hotline—across the living room floor. We'd gently take it from him and put it away. Sometimes he'd ask about Bruce's things, but he never asked where Bruce was.

One day he asked if Bruce was coming home for a holiday dinner and I gently explained that his uncle was dead and wouldn't be coming home. He stood before me, arms crossed defiantly, angry that I would suggest such a thing. "Bruce isn't dead," he declared. "He's in his police car, getting the bad guys."

I tried quietly to correct him and then realized what a great job we had done keeping Bruce's memory alive.

With his pictures around the house, his mementoes, and the way we talked about him almost daily, to Troy, Bruce was still very much alive. It warmed my heart to know that this decision to have his things around us always had made such a difference. And even more, I realized that every time I shared Bruce's story and told groups or students about him, he lived. He is still influencing with everything we do in his memory.

I'll never know how many students who watched the MADD Canada 2007 multimedia show "Friday Night," which featured Bruce's story, or heard me talk about Bruce, changed their attitudes about driving impaired and decided to find a safer way home. I'll never know who read a news article and decided to change their plans. I'll never know how many politicians changed a law to keep us all safer because of what Bruce and our family suffered. I'll never know how many lives Bruce has saved simply by us sharing the story of his life and his death. Yes, Troy, you are right. Bruce is still alive, and he's still getting the bad guys.

Our journey of healing has been long and tough. Does that mean that we don't still have bad days? Not at all. But everyone connects in some way with different things that work on this journey. It can be a simple quotation that hits home, a phrase, a poem, or a speaker that seems to be talking just to you. It can change your perspective and give you hope in an otherwise hopeless world. For me, that speaker joined me at the table just before his presentation at the national victims' weekend in 2008. It was not the first time I'd heard him present. But this time, I *heard* him.

Robert and I attended our first victims' weekend not even a year after Bruce's death. Among the speakers for the weekend was Dr. Stephen Fleming. He is a specialist in the field of grieving, and no doubt spoke many wise words that weekend. Robert and I sat there and—apologies to Dr. Fleming—our hearts at that point were still so full of pain that barely a word of what he said made any impact. There was no room in our pain for explanation or reason. A few years later, at my first national victims' weekend as national president, we were lucky enough to have him at our conference again. Time had made all the difference, and we were able to absorb his message. He talked about grief in all its many forms—how we can grieve for the loss of a child, a family member, a marriage, or even a job. If we lose *anything* we can grieve. It's a part of living and a part of dying. Grief is as varied as we are. And so is healing.

Robert and I had by this time seen many people who had dealt with their losses differently. It would raise questions for us—*Did I do things right? Is there a right way? A wrong way? Should I be better by now? When will the pain end? Am I going to get over it? Am I normal? What should I expect and what is normal? Will I survive?*

His words answered all these questions and more. He talked about accepting loss. I guess I'd always had a problem with that wording because I felt that I'd never accept Bruce's senseless death—and Dr. Fleming offered a more appropriate term. He suggested that I can be *resigned* to Bruce's death. I don't need to approve or even like it, but I can acknowledge that it has happened and that I will have to endure this tragedy. That worked for me.

And then there is the term "normal," another fallacy. There is no normal in grief; everyone grieves differently and their solutions for handling their grief are different. What works for you may not help me. I may be able to function in a week, a month, or a year. You may take more time. There is absolutely no timetable for grief.

He talked more about the different myths associated with grief, like the timeline that so many assume is the normal progression of grieving, and the belief that we will "get over it." Getting over it will never be a part of my personal experience, although I can say that time has made the pain less severe, less intense, less debilitating. But I will never "get over it."

It's also often said that marriages don't survive the loss of a child. It was great to hear from Dr. Fleming that this, too, is a myth. Statistics show that couples in good relationships do survive, and often, as they cling to each other in their shared grief, they grow stronger. This was a relief to hear. I knew that Robert's grief was very different from mine and wondered if those differences might fracture our relationship. I had MADD Canada as a support system, but Robert hadn't become a member and chose to handle his grief privately. Often that grief turned to bitterness and anger and ultimately to depression. How could it not? He had lost his only son, and although Robert's love for all our children and grandchildren is absolute, he had looked forward to a lifetime of shared interests with Bruce, and that was taken away. The devastating loss and void in his future weighed heavily on his mind. I was there for my husband, but I couldn't make Robert feel better any more than he could heal me. We each had our own journey, our own path. It is still a work in progress. In the end, although our journeys are different, we will survive as one. We depend on each other every day and neither of us does well without the other. It's just the way it is.

Then Dr. Fleming addressed my favourite term, "closure," which implies that there's an end to grief. Our loss of Bruce will be forever. There is no end, and I know that twenty years from now it will still hurt to go to the cemetery, to see Bruce's friends with their families, to look at his pictures, or just feel his presence. Tell the crash victim who has been permanently injured about closure. Dr Fleming is right. The term "resignation" is much better.

The part of Dr. Fleming's presentation that affected me the most was the section on legacy. He prompted us all to ask certain questions of ourselves, related to our own losses. So for me, the questions were as follows.

What have I learned about living as a result of Bruce's death?

I've learned to value each and every day, because at the drop of a hat, the snap of a finger, everything can change or be taken away. I've learned that each day is a gift, and it is our duty to make every minute count, to make a difference in this world.

And what have I learned about loving?

That love doesn't pass with life. It can't be confined to a coffin or urn. That no matter how much time passes, I will always love my son and appreciate the little boy he was and the man he became. I've also learned that things can't wait for tomorrow. Unsaid words of love might never be said. I will never be on bad terms with my children, because life is so fragile. I could be gone tomorrow and would wish my children to have no regrets, only memories of a mother who loved them deeply and unconditionally.

And lastly, *How am I different as a result of knowing and loving Bruce?*

This question was tougher, and probably others on the outside can see differences more than I can. I know I'm richer for having known Bruce, but what is the long-term effect?

All through my life things came easily to me, albeit with hard work. Life was good. This tragedy has made me a fighter. As in nature, when a mother's young are threatened, a defense mechanism comes into play. I couldn't defend Bruce from an impaired driver, but what I can do now is limited only by my imagination. An impaired driver took what was rightfully mine—my hope and dreams for the future. The grandchildren I will never hold and love. The son I loved and needed in my life.

I can't do anything about the past, but I *can* do something about the future so that other mothers, fathers, and families will not have to feel the loss we have endured. So that other potential victims will not have to suffer their own losses.

That's why I took on the role of national president. My three-year term ended in the fall of 2010 at our leadership conference. The experience has been simply amazing, and I would not have given it up for anything—except the one thing I cannot have back.

To have stood at the sidelines as better impaired driving legislation was passed, to have worked side by side with volunteers from across Canada, to have spoken to the supporters of MADD Canada and sometimes convert those who were not supporters, to have thanked those who support us with their donations and those who support us by calling 911 or making their own personal pledge to sober driving, to have helped others who have lost loved ones know that tomorrow will get better or those who have been injured know that they are not alone, and, I hope, to have helped to make this country a better place to live—all of it has been a gift. I am thankful for so much in these past years.

It has been a time of fighting back. Of making Bruce's life and death mean something to others. And ultimately it has been a time of healing. There is still much to do. For all of us. That presentation from Dr. Fleming did much more to help me understand the course of my healing and self-perception than any other one thing.

Other inspiration has come from a special friend, Audrey, who herself lost four children. I first met Audrey while on a vacation in the south. Although about twenty years my senior, she had a positive outlook and zest for living that impressed me. Seldom would you see Audrey without a smile and a hug for those who come through her door.

I soon learned that life had not always been easy for Audrey. As a young wife and mother in the 1950s Audrey had lost four children. I can't imagine her rage at God and life's unfairness. How much should one woman have to bear?

Audrey looked around her and saw her living children and saw that life could only go forward. Yes, she grieved, but in her own way and in her own time. Sometimes she still speaks of those she has lost or mentions the birth date of a lost child, but her moment soon passes and the ready smile returns.

I've never seen a more positive and upbeat woman. When Bruce died she was one of the first on our doorstep with food and a hug. She knew exactly what we were going through and let us know that she was there in our time of need. Her friendship and guidance have been a gift.

Despite everything that has happened to me, I have been so blessed. With the inspiring women in my life that have served as role models;

with the family I have and the love and support that comes from my husband, Robert. This has not been an easy time for him and I could never have done it without his help.

As I took on the role of national president, my daughter Jeanette told me that it would be my tribute to Bruce. That's what I thought at the time, but I've learned something. My time as national president and MADD Canada itself have been Bruce's gifts to me.

From that first contact with MADD Canada and the kind words that followed, to the insight of this organization to know what I needed to heal even before I knew it myself and that contact with other victims at our national victims' weekend so that I knew that I was not alone. MADD Canada gave me people like Dr. Fleming and others who have guided me on a path to my own healing. They gave me the ability to reach others so that I too could make a difference by sharing Bruce with them. They gave me a voice to speak for all victims of impaired driving so that they too are not forgotten.

MADD Canada has given me the greatest gift of all: hope. At a time when all I could see was the past, they gave me a vision of a brighter tomorrow and a belief that, in spite of everything, the best is yet to come. I am committed to reducing impaired driving in our country, but if I can choose one more goal for my life, it will be this: to pass on this gift, the gift that has saved my life and given it meaning after I thought all was lost. To anyone who believes that their lives will never be bright again, I want to give this precious gift of hope.

In closing, I'd like to share a poem my daughter Monica wrote for Bruce and read at his funeral.

To Bruce

Just one more time for you to call me late at night
Just one more time to get into a fight
Just one more time to hear your voice
Just one more smile
Just one more laugh.
What I would give for another day,
I wonder what it is that I would say.
If love could change the way things are
You'd live forever and go so far.
You'd know that I am always there,
I'll always love you, I'll always care.
But love can't change the way things are.
Or heal the pain or mend your scars.
I hope that love can let you know,
All our memories, we'll never let go.
Even when you're not in sight,
You're in my thoughts
Both day and night.
Love is what will keep you there
And make me thankful for all we shared.
Once one of three,
Now one of two
The missing piece, my baby brother, is you.
What I would give for another day,
I know what I would say,

I Love You

ACKNOWLEDGEMENTS AND FURTHER READING

I would like to acknowledge those who have bravely shared their experiences and loved ones with us in the hope of making change.

Please remember:

Brenda Adams, injured
Donald Sinclair King, March 13, 1925–September 6, 1993
Matthew Rodney Churchill, July 14, 1989–March 28, 2005
Alexander Gideon Fleming, May 19, 2008–October 14, 2008
Roger Linehan, July 22, 1968–December 26, 2008
Sharon and Ryan Mitchell, injured
Wayne Stephen Wright, April 22, 1962–June 13, 1992
Laura Leanne Newey, November 26, 1964–November 29, 2002
Jonathon William Newey, November 7, 1993–November 29, 2002
Bonnie Raven Dawn Louie, October 6, 1989–October 13, 2007
Matthew Alexander Block, February 14, 1991–November 1, 2003
Kevin Daniel Block, March 31, 1986–November 23, 2007
Greg O'Dell, July 13, 1973–October 29, 2006
Laura McNulty-O'Dell, January 27, 1970–October 29, 2006
Robert "Bruce" Miller, October 18, 1977–May 16, 2004

More from Dr. Stephen Fleming can be found in the book *Parenting After the Death of a Child: A Practitioner's Guide* (Routledge, 2010).
I also recommend the book by Thomas C. Badcock, *Grieving Hearts Talk: The Matthew R. Churchill Story* (Downhome Press, 2007).

Contacting MADD Canada

To reach Gloria Appleby, Victim Services Manager, call 1-800-665-6233, extension 222.

To make a donation, visit MADD Canada online or contact Mandy Msuta at 1-800-665-6233, extension 221.

www.madd.ca